Reviews of 300 San Diego County and Tijuana restaurants—

- Where to find the best pizzas
  (see p. 104)

- Elegant high tea (see p. 114)

- The best Southern cooking
  (see p. 121)

- Music with dinner (see pp. 15, 18, 66, 67, 70)

- Inexpensive hearty breakfasts (see pp. 42, 55, 59, 72, 100, 110, 112)

- The Italian Renaissance (see pp. 14, 18, 20, 39, 67, 77, 85, 86)

- The best steaks (see pp. 20, 67)

These are just a few examples of the type of information you'll find in the newest book by Eleanor Widmer, honest and outspoken restaurant reviewer for *The Reader* since 1974.

ELEANOR WIDMER

Smart Dining
in
San Diego and Tijuana

An Honest Guide to 300 Restaurants

1995

DEDICATION

To the next generation: my grand-daughters
Tanya and Shawna

And to loved ones now gone:
Fred Davis; Bruce Edelstein; Karl Keller;
Madeleine Kumler; Marvin Ladin; John Welsh.

Cover design by Brian McMurdo

Typesetting and maps by Brian Ritter

CONTENTS

NOTE

Price Ranges used in this book are defined as follows:

Low	dinner to $10
Moderate	$10-$16
Expensive	over $16

ABBREVIATIONS

AE	American Express
CB	Carte Blanche
DC	Diners Club
MC	MasterCard
V	Visa

A few other cards listed where appropriate

ACKNOWLEDGEMENTS

It would have been impossible to prepare this volume without the loving support of the *Reader*, in which most of these reviews appeared originally. Beyond that are 20 years of friendship and shared goals with Jim Holman, the publisher, and Howard Rosen, the operations director.

I am deeply grateful to those who help me with my work and whose devotion illuminates my life: Soledad and David Mosqueda; Cornelia McNeal; Saretta Holler; Susan, Hernando and Rodrigo Rivera. Special thanks to my extraordinary team of doctors: Alan Blank; James Blasingame; Leland Fitzgerald; John Hassler; Edward Iliff; Stephen Nozetz. But most especially a deep bow to Donley McReynolds.

INTRODUCTION

This book is the culmination of 20 years of work as the restaurant critic of San Diego's weekly *Reader*. During that period I've dined at 3,000 restaurants, always entered anonymously, and without fail paid for my own meals. No restaurant can pay for favorable reviews or to be included in this book. Hence the phrase, "honest guide." All opinions expressed in this volume are my own.

Diners frequently request the use of the star system in rating restaurants. I have an almost superstitious fear of them. The restaurants business is extremely volatile. Chefs who are responsible for the reputation of a restaurant suddenly move to another city. Owners decide to change concepts. Getting the food to the table at the same level of quality night after night is one of the most difficult things for a restaurant. Just consider your own experience in discovering a restaurant that you found so wonderful only a few months ago is now mediocre. Then you'll realize why the star system may be misleading. Its place in the heavens shifts too quickly.

Some of your favorite restaurants may not appear here. Be patient. They may be listed the next time.

San Diego has witnessed an incredible growth in restaurants and in its culinary sophistication. This is particularly true downtown and in the outlying suburbs of Escondido, Santee, La Mesa, Bonita, and Coronado. Every kind of American and ethnic food may be found in San Diego county, and the food preparation is of such a high level that we are no longer the poor relation of Los Angeles and San Francisco.

Here are a few tips by which I abide:

Always call for reservations; if you can't arrive, extend the courtesy of canceling. Remember that hours, prices, and menus change without notice.

Don't be intimidated by expensive dining rooms or posh locations. There's no rule that says you can't make a meal from a few appetizers, or a first course and salad. In addition, you may order the least expensive entrée on the menu or share an entrée. Even if the restaurant charges you a few dollars for an extra plate, it's worth it.

Expect competent and attentive service. If the service is fine but the food is not, don't penalize the waitperson by not leaving a tip.

Never put food into your mouth that doesn't look or smell good. Trust your instincts. Don't be embarrassed to send food back.

Restaurants thrive on genuine assessments; disclaim when necessary, but praise when you've enjoyed yourself.

Dining out is more than appeasing hunger. It provides solace, elevates morale, and serves as entertainment. May this book prepare you for days and nights of drama and laughter.

Eleanor Widmer
La Jolla, 1994

Smart Dining
in
Downtown

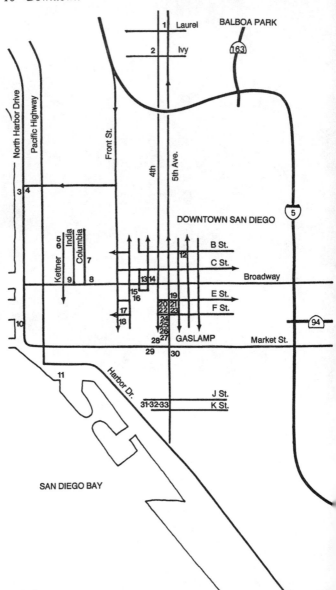

Open hours, menus, and prices change without notice. *Always call first.*

Map not exactly to scale.

Alizé
Caribbean

Paladion Building, 777 Front Street
San Diego 92101
234-0411

Sun-Th 11:30-2:30, 5:30-10:30; F-Sat 11:30-2:30, 5:30-11
Closed Christmas, New Year's Day · Full bar
Reservations recommended · Validated parking under building
All major credit cards · Upper moderate to expensive

Don't miss this luxurious dining room at the top of the building with its fixed price four-course meals. Price range from $18.50 to $26.50. The food has French influences and Caribbean spices. Dinners include appetizer, choice of soup or salad, entrée, and dessert. Stunning presentation and excellent value.

Signature Dishes: Shrimp; seafood; lobster; steak; and lamb.
Dining Tip: Great place for à la carte lunch with indoor or outdoor seating. Highly civilized and exciting.

Anthony's Star of the Sea Room
Fish/seafood

1360 North Harbor Drive (at Ash)
San Diego 92101
232-7408

Daily 5:30-10:30 · Coat for men
Closed major holidays and July 4 · Full bar
Reservations needed · Valet parking in front (ACE)
All major credit cards · Expensive

For sheer variety and items brought from all over the U.S., few restaurants can equal this major, long-lived fish and seafood house with its hard-to-find specialties. Magnificent harbor view and cart service.

Signature Dishes: *Coquille Véronique* (lobster with grapes); clams Genovese; scampi Italiano (over pasta); broad-bill swordfish; loin of swordfish; Florida pompano; petrale sole (when available); cioppino; abalone when in season. **Dining Tip:** Make reservations 24 hours in advance. Since the appetizer list is extensive, you're not obliged to order an entrée.

Athens Market
Greek

109 West F Street
San Diego 92101
234-1955

Daily 11:30-11 or later
Closed major holidays
Reservations accepted
All major credit cards

Full bar
Street parking
Low to upper moderate

Without doubt the best Greek restaurant in San Diego, it's characterized by its high spirits, vivacious owner, dedicated staff and high-quality food.

Signature Dishes: Lentil soup (a must), hobo salad, appetizers in puff pastry, baked chicken, Greek-style baked fish and any of the lamb dishes; superb custard "pie" and rice pudding. **Dining Tip:** Call in advance if you want take-out dinners. Belly dancers F and Sat.

Bayou Bar and Grill
New Orleans/Cajun

329 Market Street
San Diego 92101
696-8747

M-Sat 11:30-3, 5-10 (F and Sat till 11); Sun continuous service
    11:30-10
Closed major holidays
Reservations encouraged
All major credit cards

Full bar
Street parking
Moderate to expensive

Excellent, authentic New Orleans and Cajun fare. The food is subtle but flavorful. Contemporary setting and concerned service.

Signature Dishes: Duck esplanade; two preparations of trout; smoked pork chop with jalapeño corn bread stuffing; crawfish étouffée; seafood gumbo; Mardi Gras pasta with shrimp and crawfish; soft-shell crabs; bread pudding. **Dining Tip:** Blues and jazz piano on weekends. Don't miss Mardi Gras.

Bella Luna
Capri Italian

748 Fifth Avenue (Gaslamp)
San Diego 92101

239-3222

Daily 11:30-2:30, 5:30 to 11
Closed major holidays
Reservations recommended
AE, MC, V

Wine and beer
Valet parking with La Strada,
or fee lot on corner
Moderate

The name means beautiful moon, and the moon decor as well as recipes from the isle of Capri, Italy, are sure to please.

Signature Dishes: Eggplant patties; ravioli stuffed with fresh ricotta and marjoram, gnocchi (potato dumplings); pappardelle (broad noodles) with fresh salmon and leeks; chicken rolled with fontina cheese and ham; salmon Spinoza; rack of lamb. Don't miss the tiramisu and semi-freddo desserts.

Bravo Bistro
Portuguese, Spanish

895 Fourth Avenue (Gaslamp)
San Diego 92101

234-8888

M-F 11:15-2:30, 5-10 (F till 12); Sat 5-12; Sun 5-10
Closed Christmas, New Year's Day
Reservations accepted
All major credit cards

Full bar
Horton Plaza parking
Low to upper moderate

This charming dining room features specialties from Portugal, Spain, and France. But dishes you enjoy on one occasion may not be available the next.

Signature Dishes: Chicken Sardinia prepared with goat cheese and pine nuts; Portuguese *cataplan* (seafood stew); pork stew with clams; paella; shrimp in garlic sauce with touch of tomato; filet mignon with Roquefort sauce; salmon in parchment paper.
Dining Tip: Outdoor patio is pleasant for lunch.

Cerveceria Santa Fe
Mexican

600 West Broadway (at India), American Plaza Building
San Diego 92101   696-0043

Daily 11-11
Closed Easter, Thanksgiving, Christmas   Full bar
Reservations for 8 or more   Validated parking
All major credit cards   Low to moderate

Unique Mexican fish and seafood almost jumps from your plate
with freshness. Preparations are similar to those found in
Mexico, with 65 items on the menu. Excellent service, outdoor
patio, separate take-out area.

Signature Dishes: Puerto Penasco shrimp (cooked in lime
juice); cold seafood combination platter; shrimp or fish
enchiladas; whole fish, deep fried; filets in various sauces;
special children's menu. **Dining Tip:** Excellent low-cost meal is
Caesar's salad plus seafood soup. Don't miss the killer
margaritas.

Croce's
American/International

802 Fifth Avenue (Gaslamp)
San Diego 92101   233-4355

Daily 7:30 am-2 am   Full bar
Closed Thanksgiving, Christmas   Priority seating; call ahead
Valet in evenings $4 (subject to change) or Horton Plaza
      parking—validated at Croce's Coffee House in Horton Plaza
All major credit cards   Low moderate to expensive

The prize-winning chef does wonders with fish and seafood, and
since the eclectic menus change constantly, you're sure to
experience culinary surprises. Nightly jazz adds to the lively
atmosphere.

Signature Dishes: Norwegian salmon with vegetables; salmon
Wellington (in puff pastry); lightly breaded halibut with a sautéed
prawn; Thai chicken pasta. **Dining Tip:** Make a meal from two
appetizers. Dine early if you enjoy conversation. Outdoor dining
fun on weekends.

Dakota Grill and Spirits   American and Western
901 Fifth Avenue (Gaslamp)
San Diego 92101   234-5554

M-F 11:30-3, 5-10 (F till 11); Sat 5-11; Sun 5-9   Full bar
Closed Easter, Christmas   Street, lot, validated parking Th, F, Sat
    phone for other holidays   All major credit cards, no DC
Weekend reservations needed   Low to upper moderate

If you enjoy barbecued or rotisserie items you'll love this
Western restaurant with strong touches of Southwestern flavors.
The more romantic spot is upstairs overlooking Fifth Avenue.
Attentive service, huge portions.

Signature Dishes: Black bean soup; Caesar salad; garlic pizza
bread with cheese and sweet onions topped with whole bulb of
garlic; barbecued baby back ribs; cowboy steak. Rotisserie
chicken is a best bet. **Dining Tip:** Read the menu carefully so
you don't choose the same flavors or side dishes twice.

Dobson's   California/French
956 Broadway Circle
San Diego 92101   231-6771

M-W 11:30-10; Th-Sat 11:30-11
Closed major holidays   Full bar
Reservations recommended   Validated parking for lot in evening
AE, DC, MC, V   Moderate to expensive

Upstairs is the place to sit at this well-established
California-French restaurant. Impeccable service.

Signature Dishes: Mussel bisque (for which this restaurant is
justly famous) topped with a mile-high crust; cold fresh salmon
salad on spinach; sea scallops risotto; grilled salmon with
lemon-dill shrimp; mixed grill with venison; bouillabaisse;
sweetbreads in Madeira sauce. **Dining Tip:** Lunch (very good
salads and hamburgers) is often a madhouse around noon; arrive
after 1:30 pm for more privacy.

The Fish Market
Fish/seafood

750 North Harbor Drive
San Diego 92101

232-3474

Daily 11-10; Top of the Market Sun brunch 10-3   Full bar
Closed Thanksgiving, Christmas   All major credit cards
Top of the Market reservations   Metered parking during day,
     accepted; Downstairs 8 or more   free parking at night
Downstairs: low to moderate; Top of the Market: moderate to expens.

A huge restaurant with a harbor view, The Fish Market offers a fresh fish market, a sushi room, an oyster bar, and a moderately priced restaurant downstairs. A gourmet room, Top of the Market, exists upstairs.

Signature Dishes: Downstairs, main floor: separate sushi bar is the best downtown; oyster bar; garlic prawns with pasta; mesquite broiled swordfish; Chilean white sea bass; cioppino. Top of the Market: grilled ahi; Mexican prawns; linguine with smoked trout; Duckett in a bucket (steamed cockles); green mussels; black mussels; Manila clams. **Dining Tip:** The downstairs room serves good fresh items in a casual atmosphere; Top of the Market offers more elaborate service and unique dishes.

Grant Grill
Continental

U. S. Grant Hotel, 326 Broadway
San Diego 92101

239-6806

M-F 11:30-2, 5-10 (F till 10:30); Sat 5-10:30; Sun 5-10
Closed major holidays   Full bar
Reservations recommended   Fee valet parking, self parking garage
All major credit cards   Moderate to expensive

Designated one of the 25 best hotel dining rooms in the United States, it now boasts a new European chef. Just entering the lobby makes your spirits rise. The dining room is dark wood with large banquettes and an open kitchen.

Signature Dishes: Pacific roasted lobster tail with angel hair pasta; Coho salmon with wild mushrooms; baked filet of white sea bass with macadamia crust; rack of lamb; filet mignon; chicken with feta cheese in raspberry sauce. **Dining Tip:** F and Sat, prime rib of beef is $14.25. All meats do well here, as do the fresh fish. Very fine high tea, Tu-Sat 3-6 pm.

La Strada
Northern Italian

702 Fifth Avenue (Gaslamp/at Fifth and G)
San Diego 92101   239-3400

M-F 11:30-4:30, 5:30-11:30 (F till 12:45); Sat ??-??; Sun 5:30-11:30
Open all holidays   Full bar
Reservations accepted   Valet parking
All major credit cards   Low to upper moderate

Northern Italian food from Florence and Tuscany includes pastas, salads, and grilled fresh fish. Every item is prepared from scratch. The service is excellent and the interior highly pleasing.

Signature Dishes: Gnocchi with porcini mushrooms appetizer; chicken Tuscano (breasts rolled with asparagus, prosciutto and cheese); filet mignon in wine sauce; grilled fresh fish; tiramisu dessert. **Dining Tip:** Pasta dishes and fresh fish carry the day or night. Outdoor dining is exciting in summer.

Olé Madrid Café
Spanish and tapas

751-755 Fifth Avenue (Gaslamp)
San Diego 92101   557-0146

Tu-Sat 11:30-2:30, 5:30-12; Sun 5:30-12; Dancing 10 pm-2 am
Closed major holidays   Full bar
Reservations accepted   Valet parking
AE, MC, V   Low moderate to expensive

A huge Spanish restaurant, Old Madrid boasts two balconies and disco. You have to ascend a curved stairway for the best seating upstairs. The food is well prepared, but the distance from the kitchen causes some dishes to arrive lukewarm.

Signature Dishes: *Tortilla de casa* (potato and egg "pie"); *fabada* (bean and sausage soup); paella and *zarsuela* (fish stew). **Dining Tip:** The acoustics allow noise to reverberate. Many young people frequent this restaurant from 9 pm on; for a more sedate meal, dine early.

Pachanga Mexican Bar and Grill   Mexican

314 Fifth Avenue (Gaslamp/corner of K)
San Diego 92101   235-4545

Sun-Th 11-10; F-Sat 10 am-11 pm; Dancing lessons Tu-W 8:30-11;
   Th-Sat 8:30-2

Closed major holidays	Full bar
Reservations accepted	Valet parking available, also parking lots
All major credit cards	Low to moderate

The name means "happy times," and you'll enjoy this lively restaurant for its dancing instructors mid-week and dancing weekends, as well as for the food. The five-page menu offers Mexican standards that are fresh, well presented, and fairly priced. Very crowded weekends.

Signature Dishes: Albondigas soup; chicken tamales; any fajita dish (especially the vegetarian); carnitas. **Dining Tip:** The din is almost overwhelming on weekends because of the crowd and music. Dine early in the week for a more relaxed atmosphere.

Pacifica Grill and Rotisserie   American,

1202 Kettner Boulevard   Pacific Rim
San Diego 92101   696-9226

M-F 11:30-2, 5:30-10, Sat 5:30-10; Sun 5-10

Closed major holidays	Full bar
Reservations accepted	Free parking in building, valet in front
All major credit cards	Low moderate to expensive

A lively dining room features a relaxed atmosphere, personalized service, and fair prices.

Signature Dishes: Grilled salmon or grilled ahi (if you don't like it rare, have it done medium or well); rotisserie chicken; paella; mustard catfish with jalapeño sauce. **Dining Tip:** Make a light meal from diverse appetizer list.

Panevino
Tuscany Italian

722 Fifth Avenue (Gaslamp/Fifth and G)
San Diego 92101   595-7959

M-F 11:30-2:30, 5-10; Sat-Sun 11:30 am-12 mid.   Wine and beer
Call about holidays   Lot across street, valet parking at
Reservations suggested   5 every evening
All major credit cards   Moderate to expensive

Don't miss this Tuscany-style Italian restaurant with its exposed brick walls. Premises are small and always crowded, but the food will thrill you.

Signature Dishes: Outstanding pastas change nightly. When available try linguine with crab; capellini with wild mushrooms; *trenette* (noodles with spinach, basil, and string beans); ravioli stuffed with lamb; grilled chicken with chiles; swordfish with pine nuts; filet mignon; stuffed focaccia. **Dining Tip:** Order three or four pastas, divide them among your party, add a salad and a stuffed focaccia, and you'll have a great night.

Rainwater's
American

1202 Kettner Boulevard
San Diego 92101   233-5757

M-Th 11:30 am-midnight; F 11:30 am-1 am; Sat 5-1; Sun 5-11
Closed major holidays   Full bar
Reservations accepted   Valet parking/free parking garage
Major credit cards (not Discover)   Expensive

Noted for its fine steaks and chops, this attractive restaurant also serves live Maine lobster and fresh fish. It is a popular spot for out-of-towners who enjoy the second story dining room.

Signature Dishes: Kansas City strip; prime New York steak for two (24 oz. with peppercorns); chicken breast with garlic crust and mashed potatoes; meat loaf (a best seller); chocolate lasagne dessert. **Dining Tip:** Watch your costs—salads and soups are à la carte and prime steaks may be about $25. Chicken and meat loaf are within reach of almost everyone.

Romeo Cucina
Southern Italian

Pan Pacific Hotel, 402 West Broadway
Emerald Shapery Center, San Diego 92101   234-1777

M-F 11:30-3:30, 5:30-10:30; Sat-Sun 5:30-11 (or later)
Closed major holidays   Full bar
Reservations accepted   Validated valet parking
Major credit cards (not Discover)   Low to moderate

Here is food from Calabria, the southern tip of Italy. Dishes are hearty, pungent, simple in style, and with lots of tomato sauce. Very soothing atmosphere and wonderful service.

Signature Dishes: Bow-tie pasta with smoked salmon and caviar; black and white fettucine with scallops; spaghetti with black olives, capers, and mushrooms; grilled swordfish; whole sea bass in white wine; chicken with roasted garlic; pastry shell filled with vegetables; tiramisu dessert. **Dining Tip:** A fine place for conversation.

Säro Restaurant
Swedish

926 Broadway Circle (Broadway and Second Avenue)
San Diego 92101   232-7173

M-F 11-10; Sat 5-11
Closed Christmas, New Year's Day   Full bar
Reservations accepted   Parking in Spreckles Bldg. or at Horton Plaza
All major credit cards   Moderate

An unpretentious, well-lit Swedish dining room offers good food in a loving atmosphere.

Signature Dishes: Swedish meatballs; grilled gravlax with lobster-lime sauce; combination cold fish platter (creamed herring, garlic herring, smoked salmon, gravlax); chicken breast in oyster chile sauce; filet mignon in bleu cheese sauce. For dessert try gino, fresh fruit drizzled with chocolate, topped with ice cream. **Dining Tip:** Outdoor seating is congenial for snacks; indoors is preferable for dinner.

Anthony's Fish Grotto
1360 North Harbor Drive (at Ash)
San Diego 92101

Fish/seafood

232-5103

Daily 11:30-8:30
Closed major holidays
Reservations not accepted
All major credit cards

Full bar
Street parking
Low to expensive

For its fresh seafood salads, its fish and chips, and daily fresh fish specials, Anthony's still goes to the head of the class. Good-sized portions and time-honored preparation at low cost. Often noisy.

Brewski's Gaslamp Pub
310 Fifth Avenue (Gaslamp/Fifth and K)
San Diego 92101

American

231-7700

Daily 11:30-2 am
Open holidays; call for confirmation
Reservations for 5 or more
All major credit cards

Wine and beer
Street parking
Low to low moderate

Arrive between 4 and 6 pm and beer is $1, one of the appetizers is half-price, and other appetizers are $1 off. The brewery serves as a backdrop to this lively bar. The menu is multicultural and extensive, and the best bets are the sandwiches and burgers. Always crowded, especially on weekends. Dark beers are best.

Café Sevilla
555 Fourth Avenue (Gaslamp)
San Diego 92101

Spanish and *tapas*

233-5979

Sun-Th 6-10; F-Sat 6-12
Open major holidays
Reservations accepted; needed for flamenco
All major credit cards

Full bar
Street parking
Low to expensive

Funky room with sloping painted floors, dim lights, large bar. The cold and hot *tapas* (Spanish appetizers) are robust and plentiful. Try paella tapa; shrimp in garlic; garlic soup; tortilla tart (potato and egg with onions). Dinner entrées include paella; seafood stew; chicken; leg of lamb.

The Cheese Shop
American

401 G Street (Gaslamp), San Diego 92101   232-2303
2165 Avenida de la Playa, La Jolla 92037   459-3921

M-F 7-5; Sat-Sun 10-4   La Jolla: M-Sat 8-6; Sun 8-5
Closed major holidays   Beer (downtown); beer and wine (La Jolla)
Reservations not accepted   MC, V
Meter on street M-Sat (downtown); free 15-minute street   Low
    parking in front, side street unlimited (La Jolla)

These cafés offer outrageously good sandwiches on interesting
bread. Best are the Black Forest ham and roast pork. Muffins and
cookies are baked on the premises.

Fio's
Northern Italian

801 Fifth Avenue (Gaslamp/corner of F)
San Diego 92101   234-3467

M-F 11:30-3, 5-11 (F till 12); Sat 5-12; Sun 5-10   Full bar
Closed major holidays   Valet parking
Reservations recommended; made up to   All major credit cards
    4 weeks in advance   Moderate to expensive

Fio's has two stylish rooms, which are always crowded. For light
meals try the pizza bar. Fresh fish is always well prepared as are
daily pasta dishes and evening entrée specials.

Fontainebleau Restaurant
Continental

Westgate Little America Hotel, 1055 Second Avenue
San Diego 92101   238-1818

M-F 11:45-2, 6-10; Sat 6-10; Sun 10-2, 6-10
Closed major holidays   Full bar
Reservations recommended   Valet, validated parking in hotel lot
All major credit cards   Expensive

Traditional Continental meals are served in an elegant Old World
dining room. Best bets are roast beef, lamb chops, and fresh fish.
Fresh Maine lobster may be ordered in advance. Sunday brunch,
all-you-can-eat, includes caviar, omelet station, roast beef,
turkey, and many surprises. High tea 2:30-5 pm M-F for $12.
Dining Tip: Attracts mature diners and is excellent for
out-of-town visitors. Elegant brunch and high tea.

Harbor House
Fish/seafood

831 W. Harbor Dr. (Seaport Village), SD 92101 232-1141

M-F 11:30-3, 5-10 (F till 11); Sat 11:30-3, 4:30-11; Sun 10-3, 4:30-10
Open all holidays   Full bar
Reservations recommended   Validated parking for 2 hours
All major credit cards   Lunch low to mod.; dinner mod. to expensive

The two-level building and the harbor view are major attractions.
Fish and seafood predominate, but chicken, pasta, and steak are
also available. Preparations are wholesome but not original.

Karl Strauss' Old Columbia
Brewery and Grill
American

1157 Columbia Street (between B and C)   234-2739
Branch: San Diego Tech. Center, 9675 Scranton Rd.
   (Mira Mesa Boulevard and I-805)   587-2739

Downtown: M-Sat 11:30 am-midnight (F-S till 1 am); Sun 11:30-10
Branch: M-F 11;30-10; Sat open for private parties only; Sun 11:30-7
Closed major holidays   Downtown street; branch has two lots
Reservations accepted; branch weekdays only   Wine and beer
MC, V   Low to low moderate

Star attractions are the ales and beers brewed on the premises.
The Gaslamp Gold is especially good with the food: burgers, fish
and chips, grilled sausage, pastas, soup, and salad.
Dining Tip: The San Diego Tech. Center branch has a
Japanese-style garden, gorgeous surroundings, and Sunday jazz.

Kiyo's Japanese Restaurant
Japanese

531 F Street (Gaslamp), San Diego 92101   238-1726

M-F 11:30-2:30, 5-10; Sat 5-10
Closed major holidays   Wine and beer
Reservations not accepted   Street parking
AE, MC, V   Low

Warm personal service, sushi bar, fresh food, and low prices
mark this modest spot. Nicely prepared dinner entrées include
Yakisoba (noodle dish); tempura; sukiyaki; chicken tatsuta.
Dining Tip: The owner is always there for dinner, a major plus.

La Gran Tapa
611 B Street, San Diego 92101

Spanish
234-8272

M-F 11:30-10 (W till 11; Th-F till 12); Sat 5-12; Sun 2-10
Closed major holidays   Full bar
Reservations accepted   Street parking
AE, MC, V   Low to moderate

A lively, casual atmosphere perfect for a light meal. Menu highlights consist of *tapas* (Spanish appetizers), both hot and cold: shrimp in garlic butter, fresh octopus, beans with sausage, and cold potato and egg "pie." For heftier meals, share the paella, a saffron rice dish with shrimp, chicken, and ham.

La Tazza
823 Fifth Avenue, San Diego 92101

Coffeehouse
238-8010

M-F 10 am-midnight (F till 2 am); Sat 4-2 am; Sun 5-12
Closed major holidays   Wine and beer
Reservations accepted   Street or lot parking
MC, V   Low

The combined café and coffeehouse offers wine and beer as well as tea and coffee. The menu consists of lasagne, pasta salads, daily specials and desserts. Smoking at the front of the café.

Liaison
2202 Fourth Ave. (at and Ivy), SD 92101

French
234-5540

Sun-M 5-9:30; Tu-F 11:30-2:30, 5-9:30 (F till 10:30); Sat 5-10:30
Call on major holidays   Wine and beer
Reservations accepted   Street parking or pay lot
All major credit cards   Moderate to expensive

This French provincial restaurant has an à la carte menu as well as fixed-price meals ranging from $17.50 to $23.50. Dinner for $17.50 includes an appetizer plate, choice of soup or salad (try the lobster bisque or chicken curry soup), and entrées such as medallions of beef, lamb curry or chicken Jerusalem with artichokes and mushrooms.

Dining Tip: You may have an inexpensive light meal from the appetizer list, or just order salad and dessert soufflé. Beautiful patio is delightful for summer dining.

Mister A's
Continental

2550 Fifth Avenue, San Diego 92101 239-1377

M-F 11-2:30, 6-10; Sat-Sun 6-10
Closed Christmas, New Year's Day
Reservations accepted
All major credit cards

Full bar
Valet parking
Expensive

The bay and city views are as dazzling as ever, and a cadre of waiters and the luxury dining room have remained constant through the years. Fish, chicken, steak, and beef Wellington are featured.

Sfuzzi (pronounced Fuzzi)
California-style Italian

340 Fifth Avenue (Gaslamp), SD 92101 231-2323

M-Th 11:30-10; F-Sat 11:30 am-12 midnight; Sun 11-2, 4-10
Closed major holidays
Reservations accepted
All major credit cards

Full bar
Valet on F, Sat; or street parking
Low moderate to expensive

California-style light Italian dishes are prepared here, the best of which are scampi, vegetarian-cheese lasagne, angel hair pasta, and grilled salmon. High-intensity atmosphere, swift service, attractive clientele. Low-cost appetizers at the bar. Sit-down brunch on Sunday ($14.50) includes a drink, antipasti, entrée, dessert, and coffee.

Dining Tip: Best bet for light Sunday brunch downtown.

Yolie's Brazilian Steak House
Brazilian

815 Fifth Avenue (Gaslamp), SD 92101 696-6262

M-Sat 11-11; Sun 5-10
Open all holidays
Reservations accepted
All major credit cards

Full bar
Valet or street parking
Moderate to expensive

The only Brazilian steak house in the city. A grilled special with repeat portions ($20.95) consists of soup or salad, grilled chicken, turkey wrapped in bacon, sausage, tri-tip steak, sirloin steak, leg of lamb, tenderloin of pork, plus a platter of vegetables, rice, and polenta. Carvers bring skewers of meat or fowl to your table. The concept is novel, the food average.

Smart Dining
in
Uptown

Balboa Park
Banker's Hill
Hillcrest
Mission Hills
Mission Valley
Old Town
Uptown

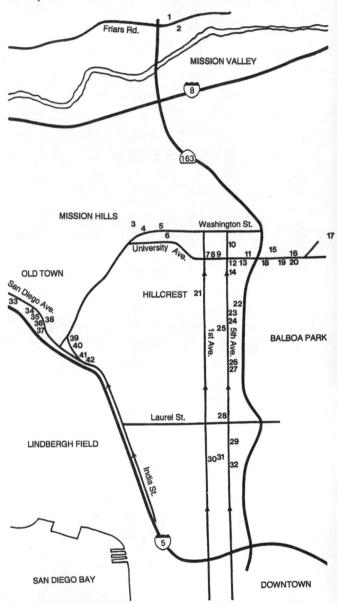

Open hours, menus, and prices change without notice. *Always call first.*

Map not exactly to scale.

Banzai Cantina
Mexican/Pacific Rim

3667 India Street (Mission Hills)
San Diego 92103   298-6388

M 11-9; Tu-Th 11-10; F 11-11; Sat 12-11; Sun 12-9;
    bar open to 2 am F, Sat
Reservations recommended on weekends   Full bar
Call about holidays   Street parking (free on weekends)
All major credit cards   Low to moderate

This crossover restaurant serves Mexican-American and Pacific Rim food. Service is fast, the atmosphere soothing, the prices affordable. Full of surprises.

Signature Dishes: California sushi; shrimp with Chinese black beans; New Mexican fettucine with seafood; Japanese bouillabaisse (clams, mussels, shrimp, fish in miso broth); semi-boned Peking-style duck with stir-fried vegetables and fried rice; carne asada. **Dining Tip:** Sit upstairs for greater quiet and intimacy.

Buccaneer's Club
French, Polish

2375 San Diego Avenue (Old Town)
San Diego 92110   299-6527

M-Sat 11:30-2:30, 5-10
Closed Easter, Christmas, New Year's Day   Wine and beer
Reservations accepted   Street parking
No credit cards   Low moderate to moderate

Seek out this eclectic dining room that seats about 30. Every item is made from scratch. The soups are Polish, the entrées are French.

Signature Dishes: Appetizers: Russian *blinis* (pancakes) with caviar; scallop mousse; escargot in cream sauce; dill pickle soup; cold or hot beet soup. Entrées: Norwegian salmon in watercress sauce; stuffed breast of chicken; rack of lamb. Dessert fruit soufflés are a must. **Dining Tip:** M-Th fixed price dinner for $13 includes soup, salad, and excellent entrée.

Busalacchi's Ristorante
Sicilian Italian

3683 Fifth Avenue
San Diego 92103
298-0119

M-F 11:30-2:15, 5-10; F-Sat 5-11; Sun 5-10
Closed Easter, Thanksgiving, Christmas, New Year's Day   Full bar
Reservations suggested   Valet parking, free at lunch time
All major credit cards   Low to moderate

If you like old-fashioned Sicilian-style cooking—tons of tomato sauce, olive oil, and garlic—then try this restaurant in a converted cottage. Sauces tend to be heavy and rich.

Signature Dishes: Seafood pasta (shrimp, scallops, mussels); swordfish stuffed with shrimp; chef's chicken (breast rolled with cheese and ham, topped with white sauce and fresh tomatoes); pasta and eggplant. **Dining Tip:** To obtain best seating, arrive early or dine mid-week. Crowded weekends.

Café Pacifica
Fish/seafood

2414 San Diego Avenue (Old Town)
San Diego 92110
291-6666

M-F 11:30-2, 5:30-10; Sat-Sun 5:30-10
Call about holidays   Full bar
Reservations recommended   Valet parking
All major credit cards   Moderate to expensive

One of the best fish houses in the city, with many Pacific Rim items. Excellent service; pleasant surroundings. Class act.

Signature Dishes: Salmon cakes; shrimp ravioli; grilled sea scallops with warm spinach; seared ahi with shiitake-ginger sauce; grilled sea bass; spinach-cheese tortellini. **Dining Tip:** Fixed price dinners, served 5:30-6:45 pm, include soup or salad, entrée, dessert, and beverage. Also note the low-fat, low-calorie items in the "Spa Menu."

California Cuisine
California

1027 University Avenue (Uptown/Hillcrest)
San Diego 92103   543-0790

Tu-F 11-10; Sat-Sun 5-10
Closed Thanksgiving, Christmas, New Year's Day   Wine and beer
Reservations recommended   Street parking
All major credit cards   Moderate to expensive

The cooking here has never been better. Presentation is ravishing;
and every dish is fresh, innovative, and wonderful to the palate.
Menus change daily. You'll enjoy the contemporary setting and
the fully enclosed, heated patio. Over 100 wines.

Signature Dishes: Pork tenderloin scallopine (layers of pork,
wild rice, and shiitake mushrooms); baked chicken breast with
feta and jalepeño yogurt; warm chicken salad; baked Alaskan
halibut with passion fruit vinaigrette; lamb with black pepper
crust and creamy polenta. **Dining Tip:** Don't miss the fixed
price meal, Tu nights, for $12.95; appetizer or salad, entrée with
vegetables, dessert. Arrive early to avoid wait. Must have
reservation for Tu dinner.

Canes California Bistro
California eclectic

Uptown District (end of Vermont, north of University)
San Diego 92103   299-3551

M-Th 4:30-10; F 11:30-11; Sat 10:30-11; Sun 10-10
Closed major holidays   Full bar
Reservations recommended   Free parking
All major credit cards   Low to low moderate

Operated by Piret and George Munger, this casual dining room
offers gourmet pizzas, pastas, and California cuisine.

Signature Dishes: Cabbage pie; Piret's salad (romaine, three
cheeses, and bacon); grilled lamb with spinach and linguine;
grilled hamburgers, served with chile sauce or sun dried
tomatoes; grilled duck breast in Dijon sauce. Patio barbecue
every W night, May through October. **Dining Tip:** The outdoor
seating area is especially pleasant and lively. Saturday breakfast
à la carte. Sunday all-you-can-eat buffet brunch plus à la carte
and lunch items.

Celadon
Gourmet Thai

3628 Fifth Avenue (Hillcrest)
San Diego 92103 295-8800

M-F 11:30-2, 5-10; Sat 5-10
Closed Thanksgiving, Christmas, New Year's Day Wine and beer
Reservations accepted Street parking
AE, MC, V Low to moderate

Celadon pioneered gourmet Thai food served in elegant
surroundings. Decor, service, and cuisine are uniformly
appealing. The menu is extensive and new items are constantly
being added, some not found elsewhere in the city. An exciting
dining experience.

Signature Dishes: Shrimp wrapped in egg noodles; heaven roll
(vegetables in rice paper); gold triangle (egg roll skin filled with
crab meat, shrimp, and cheddar); *pad Talay* (seafood in very
spicy chile sauce); heavenly lotus (cabbage leaves filled with
chicken, shrimp, snow peas); jungle vegetables in curry sauce
(highly spicy). **Dining Tip:** This may be the only Thai restaurant
that prepares marinated then grilled skinless chicken breast with
lemon grass served over a bed of lettuce. You may ask for a sweet
version.

Chilango's Mexican City Grill
Mexico City

142 University Avenue (Hillcrest) Mexican
San Diego 92103 294-8646

Sun-Th 11-9; F-Sat 11-10
Closed half day Christmas Eve and New Year's Eve, all
 day Christmas and New Year's Day No alcohol
Reservations not accepted Street parking
No credit cards Low

Looking for a bargain restaurant with tasty food? Try Chilango's.
Same menu available from opening to closing; food is served on
paper plates with plastic utensils. Six tables only. All dishes
available for take-out.

Signature Dishes: Daily soups; chicken quesadilla with special
barbecue sauce; baked tortillas topped with mushrooms, melted
cheese, and green salsa; tamales in mole sauce; Azteca special
(grilled beef, chicken, or pork). **Dining Tip:** Arrive at off hours
to avoid waiting.

Crest Café
American

425 Robinson Avenue (Hillcrest)
San Diego 92103
295-2510

Daily 7 am-12 midnight
Closed Thanksgiving, Christmas
Reservations not accepted
All major credit cards

Wine and beer
Validated lot on Fourth Avenue
Low

Signature Dishes: Onion rings served in a loaf, homemade potato chips, steak, extra-lean charbroiled hamburgers. The California chicken salad, the sandwiches, and the 10 breakfast omelets deserve particular mention. Desserts are homemade.
Dining Tip: Noisy and high spirited, this is a good spot for insomniacs.

El Indio Shop
Mexican

3695 India Street (Mission Hills), SD 92103   299-0333
Downtown Branch: 409 F Street, SD 92101   239-8151

Daily 7 am-9 pm; Downtown Branch: M-Th 11-6; F-Sat 11-8
Closed major holidays
Reservations not accepted
Discover, MC, V

Beer
Small lot (India St.) and street parking
Low

The India Street shop has an indoor dining area and outdoor patio; when these are very crowded, you may eat on benches across the street. Though it's assembly-line cooking, service is fast and food very fresh. Indoor dining downtown.

Signature Dishes: Mini-size taquitos; burritos; chimichangas (deep-fried burritos). Vegetarian: Whole wheat tortillas with beans, zucchini, cheese, and sprouts; veggie tamale (zucchini, potatoes); burrito verde (scrambled eggs, beans, sprouts, salsa).
Dining Tip: Delightful vegetarian offerings. Excellent tortilla chips.

Fifth and Hawthorn

Fish/seafood

515 Hawthorn (Uptown)
San Diego 92101

544-0940

M-T 11:30-2:30, 5-9:30; W-Th 11:30-2:30, 5:30-10; F 11:30-2:30,
    5-11; Sat 5-11; Sun 5-9:30

Closed major holidays
Reservations accepted
All major credit cards

Full bar
Street parking
Moderate to expensive

Excellent, very fresh fish and seafood dinners. Entrée price
includes soup or salad.

Signature Dishes: Salmon baked in shredded potatoes; steamed
sea bass with ginger; spicy fettucine with shrimp and scallops;
spicy calamari stir-fry. **Dining Tip:** A light meal consisting of
fish plus pasta and vegetable is available for $11.50.

The Gathering

American

4015 Goldfinch Street (Mission Hills)
San Diego 92103

260-0400

M-Th 8 am-11 pm; F-Sat 8 am-12 midnight; Sun 8 am-10 pm

Call for holidays
Reservations accepted
All major credit cards

Full bar
Street or lot parking
Low to moderate

Simple but good food is prepared at this charming café.

Signature Dishes: Charbroiled hamburger on Kaiser roll;
French onion soup; Uptown salads (greens with turkey, ham, or
roast beef; or vegetarian) served with foccacia bread; prime rib;
Maine lobster when available; fresh fish and chicken.

Dining Tip: Very hearty breakfasts are served daily outdoors or
inside.

Golden Star Restaurant

Mandarin Chinese

3761 Sixth Avenue (Hillcrest)
San Diego 92103

291-8168

M-F 11-10:30; Sat-Sun 12-10:30
Open all major holidays
Reservations accepted
Discover, MC, V

Wine and beer
Street parking
Low to moderate

The exuberant presence of Mei Ling, the owner, the many original dishes, and the low costs make this a winner.

Signature Dishes: Casseroles with lobster, seafood, or fish; *for wor* soup (shrimp, meat, chicken, pork, and masses of soft noodles; one order serves four); fresh Maine lobster. **Dining Tip:** Whole fresh Maine lobster served with sauce (black bean, ginger, or butter) costs $8.95-$9.95 and is one of the best buys in the city. Please call to make sure it's available.

Jack and Giulio's Spaghetti Western

2391 San Diego Avenue (Old Town)
San Diego 92110

Italian
294-2074

M-F 11:30-2, 4-9 (F till 10); Sat 12-10; Sun 12-9
Closed major holidays
Reservations for 4 or more on weekends
AE, MC, V

Wine and beer
Street parking, free lot
Low

Giulio's that you knew and loved for 30 years in Pacific Beach is now Jack and Giulio's. Top price for any entrée with salad is $10.95. A low-cost family restaurant with fresh, casual food. Outdoor patio.

Signature Dishes: Scampi Giulio; tortellini verde; chicken marsala; angel hair Mediterraneo; pasta primavera; pizza; and giant hero sandwiches. **Dining Tip:** For a light, casual meal try chicken pesto sandwich; ravioli with marinara sauce; shrimp bisque soup.

Kung Food Vegetarian Restaurant

Gourmet
vegetarian

2949 Fifth Avenue
San Diego 92103

298-7302

M-F 11;30-5, 5-10; Sat-Sun 8:30-1 (brunch), 1-5, 5-10
Call about holidays   Wine and beer
Reservations not accepted   Free lot
Discover, MC, V   Low to moderate

At breakfast, lunch, and dinner, vegetarian and egg dishes are available that are low in fat, salt, and cholesterol. Many entrées contain dairy products.

Signature Dishes: Quesadillas; pasta primavera; spinach-mushroom lasagne; spaghetti with mock sausage; low-fat pasta primavera; stir-fried vegetables. Low-fat desserts: Sweet potato pie; blueberry cobbler; rice pudding. **Dining Tip:** Sat or Sun à la carte brunch items are a best bet.

Montana's American Grill

American/
Southwestern

1421 University Avenue (Uptown)
San Diego 92103

297-0722

M-F 11:30-5, 5-10 (F till 11) Sat 5-11; Sun 5-10
Closed major holidays   Wine and beer
Reservations for 8 or more   Street parking, small lot
All major credit cards   Low to upper moderate

The chef does excellent work. A wide variety of smoked and grilled items. Many dishes have Southwestern influences. Contemporary decor; excellent service.

Signature Dishes: Grilled fresh fish; platter with three grilled items (enough for two people); pork stew; sausage with wild rice and black beans. **Dining Tip:** For budget dining, try first-rate soup with salad, low-cost pastas, and very tempting chili. Or, share the platter with three grilled items.

Monsoon
Vegetarian

3975 Fifth Avenue (Hillcrest/next to Landmark Theater)
San Diego 92103   298-3155

Sun-Th 10-10; F-Sat 10-11
Call about holidays   No alcohol
Reservations not accepted   Garage parking with validation
MC, V   Low

Surely one of San Diego's most delightful vegetarian restaurants.
One wall simulates a colorful rain forest; the other is devoted to
a steam table offering soups, salads, curries, and a variety of
specialties. These specialties may have Indian influence, or
Mexican or American. Most will delight you, including the fruit
smoothies and exotic nonalcoholic drinks.

Signature Dishes: Lasagne; mock duck or mock chicken
prepared from wheat gluten and stir-fried with garlic-pepper;
pasta salad with Greek dressing; veggie pie; veggie burger.
Dining Tip: Outdoor dining area is welcome in warm weather.

Old Town Mexican Café
Mexican

2489 San Diego Avenue (Old Town)
San Diego 92110   297-4330

Daily 7 am-11 pm; bar to 1:30 am
Closed major holidays   Full bar
Reservations for 10 or more   Free parking in lot
All major credit cards   Low to moderate

A boisterous café, it's noted for excellent breakfasts, served
anytime, and for rotisserie chickens roasted at the windows.

Signature Dishes: Carnitas; rotisserie chicken; all breakfast
items: eggs; machachas; chilaquiles (layers of tortillas, hot sauce,
fried eggs). Fresh tortillas prepared in open view. **Dining Tip:**
If you like a high spirited atmosphere, attend Sat night and Sun
morning. For peace and quiet, eat during off-hours.

Prego Ristorante California Italian, regional dishes
1370 Frazee Road (Hazard Center Mall/Mission Valley)
San Diego 92101   294-4700

M 11:30-10:30; Tu-Th 11:30-11; F 11:30-12 midnight; Sat 5-12; Sun
  4-10:30

Open dinner New Year's Day, closed other holidays	Full bar
Reservations accepted	Valet parking
All major credit cards	Moderate

The dining room is glitzy, there's lots of buzz and excitement, and the same menu is available all day. Food preparation is Italian with California influences, but ask for separate menu with regional dishes.

Signature Dishes: Fettucine with scampi; pasta squares layered with pesto and cheese; rack of lamb; rib eye steak with beans; grilled chicken in olive oil and chiles; mixed grilled vegetables.
Dining Tip: Bread sticks are included with the meal; bread is à la carte. Call to find out the nights regional dinners are offered.

Thai Chada   Gourmet Thai
142 University Avenue (Hillcrest)
San Diego 92103   297-9548

M-F 11:30-2:30, 5-10; Sat-Sun 5-10

Closed major holidays	Wine and beer
Reservations accepted	Street parking
All major credit cards	Moderate

If you're searching for gourmet Thai food, remember this gracious dining room. 115 items are available, each one a feast to the eye and palate.

Signature Dishes: Appetizers: *Mee Krob* (crispy noodles with mild sweet sauce); shrimp patty with beans in cucumber sauce; steamed green mussels in chicken broth with basil served in a pot; vegetables with chicken. Entrées: *Pad Thai* (unique noodles); seafood basket lined with cabbage leaves and filled with squid, shrimp, and fish filet in red curry sauce.   **Dining Tip:** 30 vegetable items are offered, such as eggplant with basil; tofu in red or green curry; mixed vegetables.

Berta's Latin American Restaurant
Latin
American

3928 Twigg Street (Old Town)
San Diego 92110

295-2343

Daily 11-3, 3-10
Closed Christmas, New Year's Day
Reservations accepted
AE, MC, V

Wine and beer
Free parking in lot
Low to low moderate

You'll find preparations from all Latin American countries, from Argentina and Brazil to Peru. If you enjoy hot seasoning, you'll like the meat, pork, chicken, fish. Not for those who prefer their food smooth and subtle.

Café Coyote
Southwestern

2461 San Diego Avenue (Old Town)
San Diego 92110

291-4695

Sun-Th 7 am-9 pm; F-Sat 7 am-11 pm
Closed Christmas
Reservations accepted
All major credit cards

Full bar
Underground parking
Low to low moderate

A good spot for a light meal. Cuisine is modestly Southwestern. Best bets à la carte are the black bean chile, Sante Fe *posole* (chicken soup with hominy), and quesadilla with mango relish. Breakfast includes blue corn pancakes and American dishes. Cantina downstairs, 692-0802.

Chicken Pie Shops of San Diego
American

2633 El Cajon Boulevard (Uptown)
San Diego 92104

295-0156

Sun-Th 10-8; F-Sat 10-8:30
Closed Christmas, New Year's Day
Reservations not accepted
No credit cards

No alcohol
Street and lot parking
Low

You'll get lots of fried chicken, chicken and turkey pies, mashed potatoes, and desserts for prices that don't seem to have changed much since the shop opened more that 50 years ago. It's like the Fourth of July in a small town. A great bargain.

City Delicatessen
Jewish & American
535 University Avenue (Hillcrest)
San Diego 92103   295-2747

Sun-Tu 7 am-12 midnight; F-Sat 7 am-2 am
Closed Christmas, Yom Kippur   Wine and beer
Reservations for 6 or more   Off street parking
MC, V   Low to moderate

Jewish specialties include brisket of beef, chicken-in-the-pot, chopped liver, and a wide variety of sandwiches. Or try vegetarian grilled eggplant sandwich, vegetarian chili, and spinach lasagne. The food is average, but long hours are great.

Extraordinary Desserts
Bakery/Coffeehouse
2929 Fifth Avenue
San Diego 92103   294-7001

M-Th 8:30 am-11 pm; F 8:30 am-12 midnight; Sat-Sun 2-11
Closed major holidays   No alcohol
Reservations not accepted   Street parking
MC, V   Low

If you've been searching for dessert after a movie or other cultural event, this is just the spot. The baker-owner prepares sensuous cakes, tarts, cookies, and all manner of chocolate goodies. Desserts vary with the seasons; many commemorate holidays. Teas and coffees are uniformly good. In the summer, the patio is especially charming. Note the late hours.

Figaro Italian Restaurant
Neopolitan Italian
741 West Washington Street (Mission Hills)
San Diego 92103   296-4811

Tu-F 11:30-2:30, 5-9:30 (F till 10:30); Sat 3-10:30; Sun 3-9:30
Closed major holidays   Wine and beer
Reservations accepted   Street parking
All major credit cards   Low to moderate

This long-enduring restaurant offers traditional, old world, home-style meals. Many of the recipes are from Naples, Italy. The menu includes pizzas, chicken, meat dishes, and large portions of cannelloni. Good place to take the whole family.

Gelato Vero Caffe
Dessert/Coffeehouse

3753 India Street (Mission Hills)
San Diego 92103   295-9269

M-F 6 am-12 midnight (F till 1 am); Sat 7 am-1 am; Sun 7:30-12 mid.
Closed major holidays   No alcohol
Reservations not needed   Street parking
AE, over $10   Low

A fine spot for Italian sorbettos and ice creams, pastries of all
kinds, and coffee. Continental-style breakfasts—bagels,
croissants, sweet rolls, and coffee available daily. Eat upstairs for
greater comfort.

Hob Nob Hill
American

2271 First Avenue (Banker's Hill)
San Diego 92101   239-8176

Daily 7 am-9 pm
Closed Christmas Eve and Christmas Day   Wine and beer
Reservations accepted   Street parking
All major credit cards   Low

Hob Nob Hill has always led a double life. For breakfast M-F it
appeals to professionals who make deals over coffee. At night it
serves old-fashioned meals: corned beef and cabbage, fried
chicken, beef stew with dumplings, roast pork and lamb,
sauerbraten, and Waldorf salad. Specials ($9.95) come with soup
or salad, potatoes, vegetables, individual breads and muffins.

Imperial House
Continental

505 Kalmia Street (Balboa Park)
San Diego 92101   234-3525

M 11-2; Tu-Th 11-4, 5-9; F 11-4, 5-11; Sat 5-11
Closed major holidays   Full bar
Reservations accepted   Free valet parking
All major credit cards   Moderate to expensive

An excellent place for lunch, which (for about $7.25) includes
soup or salad plus hot entrée. This restaurant still serves its
traditional specialties: steak, fresh fish, Anna potatoes. Tableside
service and a charming view of Balboa Park.

Mandarin Dynasty
Mandarin Chinese

1458 University Avenue (Hillcrest)
San Diego 92103   298-8899

Daily 11-11
Call about holidays   Wine and beer
Reservations accepted   Lot parking
All major credit cards   Low to low moderate

Care to order a feast in advance for a large party? The chef needs
at least four hours notice for casserole soup, Yu Hsiang beef,
scallops in pepper, shrimp in Chinese sauce, ginger chicken,
General Tao's chicken, and Chinese broccoli in oyster sauce.
Items from the menu tend to be only average.

Mission Hills Café
California

808 West Washington (Mission Hills)
San Diego 92103   296-8010

Tu-Sun 7-11, 11-3, 5-10
Call about holidays   Wine and beer
Reservations accepted   Street parking
All major credit cards   Low

For dinner, a good bargain restaurant. Fixed price ($10)
California cuisine meals include appetizer, soup or salad, plus
entrée with vegetables and dessert. Dinner items change nightly
and range from pastas and vegetarian items to chicken, fish, or
meat. Superb bread. Breakfast served all day.

Pasta al Dente
Pasta

420 Robinson Avenue (Hillcrest)
San Diego 92103   295-2727

M-Th 11-10:30; F 11-11; Sat 12-11; Sun 12-10:30
Closed Thanksgiving, Christmas   Wine and beer
Reservations not accepted   Free parking in lot
All major credit cards   Low

All sauces, pastas, daily soups, and salads are made from scratch.
Thirty pasta dishes are available at this bright, clean,
unpretentious restaurant. Costs are low, portions are huge, and
the enterprise is marked by honesty.

Pasta Time Café

Pasta

1417 University Avenue (Uptown)
San Diego 92103   296-2425

M-Th 11-9; F-Sat 11-10; Sun 12-9
Call about holidays   No alcohol
Reservations not necessary   Street parking (metered during day)
No credit cards   Low

Though the atmosphere is casual—you order at the counter and
the food is brought on a tray—sauces are made from scratch and
pastas include salad and garlic bread. The lasagne is
commendable; for hungry bargain hunters the meatball sandwich
is filling and inexpensive (ask to have the bread toasted).

Quel Fromage

Coffeehouse

523 University Avenue (Hillcrest)
San Diego 92103   295-1600

Sun-Th 6 am-11 pm; F-Sat 6 am-12 midnight
Closed major holidays   No alcohol
Reservations not accepted   Street parking
No credit cards   Low

For light fare, such as desserts, coffee, and tea, this is a fine,
smoke-free environment in which to enjoy reading or good
conversation. A patio is available for smoking.

Rusty Pelican

Fish/seafood

5010 Mission Center Road (Mission Valley)
San Diego 92108   291-6974

M-Th 11-4, 4-10; F-Sat 11-4, 4-11; Sun (br) 10-2:30, 4-10
Open all holidays   Full bar
Reservations accepted   Valet parking at lunchtime
All major credit cards   Low moderate to moderate

Here's a modest spot for fish and seafood. Offers the same menu
as the La Jolla branch. Sunset dinners for $8.95 to $9.95 (soup
or salad, entrée, potato, vegetable, dessert, tea or coffee) are
served daily 4-6 pm. Very fresh product. Sunday, all-you-can-eat
buffet.

Saffron   Thai
3731-B India Street (Mission Hills)
San Diego 92101   574-0177

M-F 10:30-8:30; Sat 11:30-8; Sun 11-7
Closed major holidays   No alcohol
Reservations not necessary   Street parking
MC, V   Low

Very fine grilled chicken is available for take-out or may be eaten
on benches outdoors. Side dishes, such as Cambodian salad
(cabbage with peanuts) or rice paper stuffed with noodles and
vegetables, are also prepared. Excellent, healthy food with lots
of flavor. Unusual dishes prepared for Thanksgiving and
Christmas. **Dining Tip:** Phone to ask about specials.

The Second Cup   Romanian
4030 Goldfinch (Mission Hills)
San Diego 92103   692-3255

Tu-Sat 7:30 am-4 pm; F (by reservation) 5:30 am-10 pm
Closed major holidays   No alcohol
Reservations accepted F night only   Street parking, pay lot
No credit cards   Low to moderate

The city's only Romanian restaurant exists in this tiny shop that
seats about 20 people. The cooking, done by the owner's mother,
is excellent; wonderful chicken-vegetable soup, chicken
schnitzel, cabbage rolls, chicken with fresh tomato sauce, and
feathery meatballs and meat loaf. Same menu for lunch and
dinner. There is one catch: Dinner is served only on F night or
by appointment. Or you may have a late lunch at 4 pm and
consider it dinner.

Dining Tip: If you organize a party of six or more and call in
advance, the dining room will be available any evening.

Stefano's   Italian
3671 Fifth Avenue (Hillcrest)
San Diego 92103   296-0975

Sun-Th 5-9; F-Sat 5-10:30
Closed major holidays   Full bar
Reservations accepted   Street parking, pay lot
All major credit cards   Low to moderate

In business for many years, Stefano's remains a good place for
Old World-Italian cooking, especially pastas, fresh fish, and
chicken dishes. With a full entrée you may obtain a salad that
resembles antipasto for $2. Half orders for some dishes. Lovely
dining room one flight up. Some outdoor seating.

The Study   Coffeehouse
104 University Avenue (Hillcrest)
San Diego 92103   296-4847

Daily 8 am-12 midnight
Open major holidays   No alcohol
Reservations not necessary   Street parking
No credit cards   Low

An excellent, immaculate coffeehouse, decorated to look like a
study and frequented by students. Offers coffee drinks, juices,
teas, and very tasty muffins, scones, cakes, soups, salads, and
sandwiches. Seek out this place.

Taste of Szechuan   Chinese
670 University Avenue (Uptown)
San Diego 92103   291-1668

M-Th 11-3, 3-12; F-Sat 11:30-3, 3-2 am; Sun 12-3, 3-12
Open Thanksgiving; closed other holidays   Wine and beer
Reservations for 4 or more   Street parking
MC, V   Low to moderate

The Mandarin Szechuan menu offers standards with few
surprises. The three best features are the lovely room, the
astonishing friendliness of the management, and the late hours.
The Peking duck is excellent, as are the chopped chicken in
lettuce cups, and soft noodles with shrimp, beef, or chicken.

Smart Dining
in
Beach Areas

Bay Park
Five Points (Midway)
Harbor Island
Mission Bay
Mission Beach
Ocean Beach
Pacific Beach
Point Loma
Shelter Island

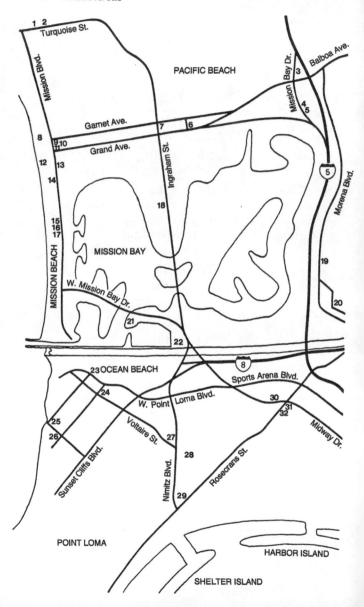

Open hours, menus, and prices change without notice. *Always call first.*

Map not exactly to scale.

Andres' Patio Restaurant   Cuban
1235 Morena Boulevard (Bay Park)
San Diego 92110   275-4114

Tu-Sat 11-9
Closed Thanksgiving; Christmas to New Year's Day   Wine and beer
Reservations accepted   Street parking
All major credit cards   Low to low moderate

San Diego's only Cuban restaurant provides a loving atmosphere
and authentic specialties. Latin groceries are available next door.
Swift service, unpretentious but clean premises.

Signature Dishes: Shredded beef in wine sauce; roast pork with
yuca and moros; chicken and rice; top sirloin. You can make a
meal from the appetizers of empanadas (pastry stuffed with meat
or chicken), Cuban *tamal* (tamales), and fried plantains.
Excellent Cuban sandwiches (roast pork and baked ham, served
hot). Extraordinary flan. **Dining Tip:** Black beans should be
poured over the entrée, not eaten separately. Puerto Rican
specialties on Friday.

Baci's   Northern Italian
1955 West Morena Boulevard (Bay Park)
San Diego 92110   275-2094

M-F 11:30-2, 5:30-10; Sat 5:30-10
Closed major holidays   Full bar
Reservations accepted   Parking in back/side
All major credit cards   Moderate to expensive

A full bar, three well-appointed rooms, superior service, and an
interesting menu characterize Baci's. Soup, salad, and appetizers
are à la carte. Food preparation remains consistently fine
throughout the years.

Signature Dishes: Appetizers: focaccia bread, squid in tangy
tomato sauce. Entrées: chicken breast with Gorgonzola cheese,
prosciutto, and wine; swordfish with bread crumb crust, baked
in white wine; *penne* with four cheeses; tortellini with three
sauces (pesto, marinara, bechamel); fettucine in Bolognese
sauce. Outstanding zabaglione dessert and tiramisu.   **Dining
Tip:** Forget calories. Dishes are prepared with butter, cheese, and
cream. It's worth it!

The Belgian Lion

Belgian

2265 Bacon Street (Ocean Beach)
San Diego 92107   223-2700

Th-Sat 5-10   Wine and beer
Call about holidays   Reservations needed
All major credit cards   Upper moderate to expensive

Without a doubt the best Belgian food in San Diego is served in this charming, provincial-style dining room. The vegetables, which include a turnip soufflé, are incomparable. This venerable dining room is not to be missed.

Signature Dishes: Cassoulet; confit of duck; salmon in sorrel sauce; Alsacian-style sauerkraut with ham and sausage. **Dining Tip:** Select soup over salad—the soups are unique. Belgian Lion provides the best wine dinners in the city. Phone to get on the mailing list.

Chateau Orleans

New Orleans/Cajun

926 Turquoise Street (Pacific Beach)
San Diego 92109   488-6744

M-Sat 6-10; Sun 5-9
Closed major holidays   Wine and beer
Reservations accepted   Free parking in front and on street
All major credit cards   Low moderate to expensive

Because of the new owner, the interior has never looked better. All dinners include house salad, a Cajun stuffed pastry, and popovers. The food is very spicy, so if you would like it less hot, be sure to say so when you order. Very large portions, commendable service.

Signature Dishes: Blackened prime rib; Cajun-style fish; red beans and rice; stuffed pork chops with fruit glaze; catfish; soft-shell crab; King salmon and scallops (prepared in French, rather than Cajun, style). **Dining Tip:** With *Reader* coupon, mid-week dinners are often two for $19.95.

China Inn

Mandarin, Szechuan, and Hong Kong

877 Hornblend St. (between Garnet and Grand)   Chinese

San Diego 92109   483-6680

Sun-Th 11:45-3, 3-10; F-Sat 11:45-3, 3-11
Call about holidays   Full bar
Reservations not necessary   Parking lot
AE, MC, V   Moderate

At least 118 items appear on the menu, which offers Mandarin, Szechuan, and Hong Kong specialties. Simple setting; outstanding food.

Signature Dishes: Sweet and pungent shrimp, fresh fish, or chicken in wine sauce; the best barbecued pork chops anywhere; Hong Kong-style shrimp. **Dining Tip:** It's worth the effort to call and speak to Andy before dining. Ordering from the menu is fine, but for a transcendent experience, place yourself in Andy's hands.

Di Roma

Italian

1845 Quivira Way (Mission Bay)

San Diego 92109   222-1189

Tu-F 11-2, 5-9 (F till 10); Sat 5-10; Sun 5-9
Closed major holidays   Wine and beer
Reservations recommended   Free parking
All major credit cards   Low to moderate

Two dining rooms are available; the one that's an enclosed porch tends to be noisy, but it has a view of the bay.

Signature Dish: Pizza, especially the stuffed pizza with top and bottom crust, which is thrilling. If you're not a pizza lover order low-cost pastas with soup or salad. **Dining Tip:** Good place to take children.

French Gourmet
French & California

960 Turquoise Street (Pacific Beach)
San Diego 92109   488-1725

M-F 11-2, 5-9; Sat-Sun 8-2, 5-9
Closed major holidays   Wine and beer
Reservations requested evenings   Street parking
All major credit cards   Low to moderate

An airy, pleasant dining room, French Gourmet serves French food with California influences. It's light, good-tasting, and easy on your purse. For dinner, you have a choice of soup or salad plus entrée with vegetable. Ravishing desserts and bakery.

Signature Dishes: Poached salmon; filet mignon; Greek-style chicken; seafood pasta; catfish in Dijon sauce. **Dining Tip:** Breakfast is very pleasant here. Try bread basket plus coffee; crepes; omelets Breakfast and lunch items served simultaneously from 11-2.

Islandia Bar and Grill
American & Continental

Hyatt Islandia Hotel, 1441 Quivira Basin (Mission Bay)
San Diego 92109   224-1234

M-Sat 5-11; Sun 9:30-2 (brunch)
Open all holidays   Full bar
Reservations accepted   Parking near restaurant/south
All major credit cards   Moderate to expensive

Noted for its view of the bay, this American and Continental dining room offers à la carte dinners that are excellent in appearance, taste, and quality.

Signature Dishes: Lobster bisque soup; first-rate crab cakes prepared without bread; braised artichoke; sautéed halibut in hazelnut sauce; swordfish steak with sun-dried tomatoes; salmon filet with rosemary sauce; spinach, endive, and spicy shrimp salad. **Dining Tip:** The Sunday brunch is almost overwhelming and always popular. It includes an omelet station, waffles, blintzes, lox, pasta, turkey, roast beef, salads, and a separate dessert table. No dinner on Sun.

Karinya Thai Restaurant
Thai

4475 Mission Boulevard (Pacific Beach)
San Diego 92109
270-5050

M 5:30-10:30; Tu-F 11:30-2:30, 5:30-10:30; Sat 5:30-10:30; Sun
  5:30-9:30

Closed Thanksgiving, Christmas	Wine and beer
Reservations accepted	Parking in lot
MC, V	Moderate

The impressive menu boasts 70 items, of which 21 are appetizers.
The room with floor seating is a knockout. Stunning presentation
and excellent preparation.

Signature Dishes: Appetizers: *mee krob* (vermicelli crispy
noodles with shrimp and sweet sauce); shrimp sarong (shrimp
with egg noodles and sweet chili sauce); bridal shrimp (shrimp
on toast). Entrées: marinated beef with broccoli; three-flavor
scallops (sweet, sour, and salty sauces mixed together); *pad Talay*
(a seafood combination with special sauce); *pad Thai* (noodles
with shrimp, chicken, and ground peanuts). **Dining Tip:** When
ordering curry, remember the green chili paste is spicier than the
red. "Very spicy" is intolerable for most Americans.

Palenque
Regional Mexican

1653 Garnet Avenue (Pacific Beach)
San Diego 92109
272-7816

M 5-9; Tu-Sun 11:30-2:30, 5-9 (F-Sat till 10)

Closed Christmas, New Year's Day	Wine and beer
Reservations for 4 or more	Free parking in rear, also across street
All major credit cards	Low to moderate

Palenque serves regional dishes from Puebla, Guerrero, Nuevo
Leon, and Mexico City. All dishes are quite spicy; if you prefer
fewer chiles, say so before ordering. Charming setting,
super-fresh food, attentive service.

Signature Dishes: Tortilla soup; pozole soup (with either green,
red, or white chiles plus chicken broth and hominy grits); from
Puebla, shredded pork with tomatoes and potatoes; from
Morelia, chicken breast with ancho chiles (very spicy). **Dining
Tip:** Make a meal from these two appetizers plus soup: tortillas
topped with beef, potatoes, and cheese; shrimp cooked in olive
and garlic. Don't miss this café.

Santa Clara Grill   American
3704 Mission Boulevard (Mission Beach)
San Diego 92109   488-9484

M-F 8 am-9 pm (F till 9:30); Sat 7:30 am-9:30 pm; Sun 7:30 am-9 pm
Closed Christmas Day; call about Christmas Eve   Wine and beer
Reservations accepted   Public parking across street
AE, DC, MC, V   Low to moderate

Here's a pleasant, well-decorated, casual dining room with a
lovely outdoor patio that's usually filled to capacity for breakfast
during the weekend.

Signature Dishes: For either lunch or dinner try the outrageous
sandwiches on sourdough bread: French dip; vegetarian; turkey
club; tuna melt. Good dinner items are faqueburgers (made from
soy beans), meat loaf with mashed potatoes and vegetables, or
fresh fish. **Dining Tip:** One sandwich is enough for two and
arrives with either home-style fries or salad. Share the sandwich
and order additional fries, salad, or dessert.

Sushi Ota   Sushi bar/Japanese
4529 Mission Bay Drive (Pacific Beach)
San Diego 92109   270-5670

M 5:30-10:30; Tu-F 11:30-2, 5:30-10:30; Sat-Sun 5:30-10:30
Closed major holidays   Wine and beer
Reservations accepted   Parking lot in shopping strip
MC, V   Low to expensive

A first-rate Japanese restaurant, Sushi Ota deserves attention,
especially for its excellent sushi bar and the 30 appetizers.

Signature Dishes: Make a meal from appetizers: smoked
salmon; crab in a French-style sauce; *gyoza* (dumplings);
asparagus rolled in beef; yellowtail; tempura. **Dining Tip:**
Arrive early to avoid a long wait for sushi. The quarters are small,
but a separate waiting room is available.

Thee Bungalow   French/Continental
4996 West Point Loma Boulevard (Ocean Beach)
San Diego 92107   224-2884

M-Th 5:30-9:30; F-Sat 5-10; Sun 5-9
Closed July 4; call about other holidays   Wine and beer
Reservations preferred   Street parking; free gravel lot
All major credit cards   Low to moderate

Located in a charming bungalow, a landmark of Ocean Beach,
this romantic restaurant offers well-prepared French/Continental
food. Miraculously, the prices are moderate. Roaring fireplace;
outdoor patio.

Signature Dishes: Roast duck; lamb shanks; sea bass; Swiss
chicken (with Westphalian ham, asparagus, and cheese); grilled
scallops with smoked tomato sauce; rack of lamb. **Dining Tip:**
Sun-Th, soup or salad, choice of seven entrées plus vegetables,
$9.95 to $10.95. Same low-cost dinners available F and Sat,
5-5:45 pm. One of the best bargains in the city.

Cucina Fresca   Northern Italian
1851 Bacon St. (Ocean Beach), SD 92107   224-9490

M 6-9; Tu-Th 11-3, 5-10; F-Sat 11-3, 5-11; Sun 11-3, 5-9
Closed Thanksgiving, Christmas   Wine and beer
Reservations accepted   Street parking
All major credit cards   Low to low moderate

This small, family-operated restaurant serves very tasty Italian
food at low cost. The lasagne Florentine is especially good, as
are the chicken dishes and individual pizzas. The low-cost
specials are fine value.

Dining Tip: Cioppino (fish and seafood stew) is the most
expensive item, but it's a treat.

D'Lish Pizza and Pasta Italian

4150 Mission Boulevard, Promenade Shopping Center
    upstairs (Pacific Beach), San Diego 92109   483-4949
Chula Vista Branch: 386 East H Street   585-1371
La Jolla Branch: 7514 Girard Avenue   459-8118

M-F 11:30-9; Sat-Sun 11:30-10   Wine and beer
Closed Christmas, New Year's Day; call about other holidays
Reservations for large parties only   Street or lot parking
All major credit cards   Low to low moderate

The pizzas and pastas are tasty; the salads are huge and fresh—one salad is enough for two people. La Jolla and Chula Vista offer full service; in Pacific Beach you order at the counter.

Fairouz Cafe and Gallery Lebanese & Greek

3166 Midway Drive (Midway), SD 92110   225-0308

M-Sat 11-5, 5-10; Sun 11-5, 5-9
Closed Thanksgiving, Christmas, New Year's Day   Wine and beer
Reservations accepted F, Sat, Sun   Free parking in lot
All major credit cards   Low to low moderate

Seek out this family-owned and -operated restaurant for wonderful Lebanese and Greek food. The owner, a noted artist, displays his paintings. The menu offers excellent lamb dishes, stuffed grape leaves, and exotic vegetarian meals. Copious all-you-can-eat buffet also available at lunch or dinner. Given 24 hours, they will prepare an astonishing low-cost Lebanese feast.

Georgia's Greek Cuisine Greek

3550 Rosecrans St. (Midway), SD 92110   523-1007

M-F 11-9; Sat-Sun 11-10
Closed Thanksgiving, Christmas, New Year's Day   Wine and beer
Reservations accepted   Free parking in the lot
MC, V   Low to moderate

Best bet is the combination plate that includes lemon soup, baked chicken, fresh spinach pie, dessert, and coffee. Also note the stuffed grape leaves, moussaka, souvlaki, beef or lamb kabobs, and roast leg of lamb. Good rice pudding.
Dining Tip: Excellent lunches under $6 are served until 4 pm.

Guava Beach Bar and Grill American
3714 Mission Boulevard (Mission Beach)
San Diego 92109   488-6688

M-Th 4-12 mid.; F 4-1 am; Sat 11 am-1 am; Sun 11 am-12 mid.
Closed major holidays   Full bar
Reservations accepted   Private lot
AE, MC, V   Low to moderate (except for lobster)

A good-looking, clean restaurant with big TVs, Guava Beach serves old-fashioned delights, such as meat loaf with mashed potatoes and macaroni and cheese in large amounts at low costs. Lobster (when available), fresh fish, and pasta dishes are also well prepared. **Dining Tip:** 15 entrées are under $10.

Kabul West Afghanistan
3555 Rosecrans (Midway), San Diego 92110   224-8200

M-Sat 11-2:30, 4-9:30
Closed July 4, Christmas   Wine and beer
Reservations accepted   Free parking
All major credit cards   Low

Family-operated Afghanistan restaurant. It offers lovely decor, pleasant food, and a top price of $11.95. Each entrée includes salad plus nan bread. Best bets are lamb with saffron rice topped with carrot strips and raisins; tandoori chicken; Afghan-style ravioli, called *aushak*; and vegetarian plate with two rices, salad.

Kolbeh Restaurant Persian
4501 E. Mission Bay Dr. (Pac. Bch.), SD 92109 273-8171

Sun-Th 11:30-9:30; F-Sat 11:30-10
Open all holidays   Wine and beer
Reservations accepted   Parking front and back
MC, V   Low to low moderate

Persian food is low in calories, good-tasting, nonfat and often charbroiled. The two best dishes, served with basmati rice, are the filet mignon and the chicken *barg* (as distinct from kabobs). With any charbroiled dish, order yogurt with cucumbers and mint plus the puréed eggplant (*borani*); the broiled items are dry without them.

Kono's
American breakfast

704 Garnet (Pacific Beach), San Diego 92109   483-1669

M-F 7 am-3 pm; Sat-Sun 7 am-4 pm
Closed Thanksgiving, Christmas   No alcohol
Reservations not necessary   Street parking; lot in back
No credit cards   Low

For an inexpensive but hearty breakfast, you can't get a better
deal. The Big Breakfast consists of eggs, pancakes, potatoes,
bacon, and English muffin for $3.75. A lunch menu (salads and
sandwiches) is also available, and hamburgers are cooked from
noon to closing.

Lamont Street Grill
American

4445 Lamont St. (Pacific Beach), SD 92109   270-3060

Sun-Th 5:30-10; F-Sat 5:30-10:30
Call about holidays   Full bar
Reservations accepted   Street parking
All major credit cards   Moderate

Dinners range from $11.95 to $14.95 and include salad or soup.
Most are chicken preparations—the Dijon chicken is a signature
dish—and are accompanied by potatoes and vegetables. An
outstanding physical feature is the real fireplace and fire in the
outdoor patio. Pleasant dining room.

Little Italy
Sicilian Italian

4204 Voltaire (Point Loma), SD 92107   225-9900
East SD Branch: 4367 University (92105)   281-4949

Daily 11 am-2 am
Closed Thanksgiving, Christmas   Wine and beer
Reservations not necessary   Low
AE, MC, V   Pt. Loma: parking in back; ESD: street parking

The Italian feast for two consists of salad, cheese pizza, lasagne,
spaghetti, and garlic bread for approximately $10, to eat there or
to go. Old-fashioned recipes include spaghetti and meatballs,
calzone, pasta dishes, chicken. Good value.

Michelangelo
Sicilian, central Italian
1878 Rosecrans Street (Point Loma)
San Diego 92106   224-9478

M-Sat 11-10; Sun 4-10
Closed Thanksgiving, Christmas   Wine and beer
Reservations accepted   Parking in front
AE, MC, V   Low to low moderate

It's best to order the full Italian dinner that includes soup or salad,
or try the evening pasta special. The scampi entrée and chicken
with eggplant are wonderful. Good pizza. Old-style cooking.

Pizzeria Uno
Italian
4465 Mission Blvd. (Pacific Bch.), SD 92109   483-4143

M-Sun 11 am-2 am
Closed Christmas   Full bar
Reservations accepted for 15 or more   Street and lot parking
All major credit cards   Low to low moderate

The expanded menu includes lots of salads and low-calorie items
as well as pizzas. The shift has been to healthier offerings, such
as pastas with light sauces. Continuous service; fine for late
night.

Que Pasa Rockin' Cantina
California-Mexican
4287 Mission Blvd. (Pacific Bch.), SD 92109   273-5076

M-Th 7 am-11 am, 11-11; F-Sat 7 am-11 am, 11 am-1 am; Sun
     (brunch) 7 am-1 pm, 1-11
Open all major holidays   Full bar
Reservations accepted for large parties   Free lot parking
AE, MC, V   Low to moderate

As its name implies, this restaurant is a "happening" place: loud
music and a gathering spot for the youthful. California-Mexican
food. The top price is $10.95. Good Chimichangas, soft-shell
tacos, swordfish fajitas. Breakfast and brunch à la carte.

Qwiig's Bar and Grill
Fish/seafood
5083 Santa Monica (Ocean Bch.), SD 92107   222-1101

M-Th 11:30-2:30, 5:30-9; F 11:30-2:30, 5-10; Sat 5-10; Sun
    10:30-2:30, 5-9
Closed Thanksgiving, Christmas   Full bar
Reservations accepted   Free underground and off-street parking
All major credit cards   Moderate

A splendid ocean view, an oyster bar, interesting salads, à la carte
Sun brunch, and fresh fish are the main attractions. Long flight
of stairs or elevator.

Saska's
Steak & seafood
3768 Mission Blvd. (Mission Bch.), SD 92109   488-7311

M-F 11:30 am-2 am (F till 3); Sat 9:30 am-3 am; Sun 9:30 am-2 am
Closed Thanksgiving, Christmas   Full bar
Reservations accepted   Lot parking for fee
All major credit cards   Low to moderate

Saska's, with its beachcomber atmosphere, is the perfect spot for
insomniacs. Hearty breakfasts of carne asada and eggs, or pork
chops and eggs, are served from 11 pm to 1 am; to 3 am F and
Sat. Steak lovers shouldn't overlook the prime beef "Saska
steak," while nightly fresh fish is a good choice for lighter fare.
Sat and Sun à la carte brunch offers American and Mexican
specialties.
Dining Tip: Two-for-one dinners frequently available, but you
must have a *Reader* coupon.

Sheldon's Café
American
4711 Mission Bay Dr. (Pac. Bch.), SD 92109   273-3833

Daily, 24 hours a day
Open all major holidays   Wine and beer
Reservations not accepted   Lot parking
MC, V   Low

Although the old favorites—chicken-fried steak, fried chicken,
old-fashioned croquettes, and liver and onions—are still on hand,
the menu has been revised toward healthier dining. All
vegetables are fresh, fresh fish appears daily, and the breakfast
buffet offers lots of fresh fruit. Open 62 years; going strong.

Tosca's Pasta and Pizza   Italian
3780 Ingraham Street (Pacific Beach)
San Diego 92109   274-2408

Summer: Daily 11:-11; Winter: Daily 12-9 (F-Sat till 10)
Open all holidays   Wine and beer
Reservations not necessary   Street parking
All major credit cards   Low

The soup, served in a hard roll, is delightful and so are the pasta dishes, especially the *quatratini* (pasta with fresh spinach in Alfredo sauce). Pizzas include 7 cheeses, forest mushroom, smoked salmon, or Californian with vegetables and cheese. Fabulous salads. All portions mammoth.

The Venetian   Sicilian Italian
3663 Voltaire St. (Pt. Loma), SD 92106   223-8197

M-F 11-9:30 (F till 10); Sat 4-10; Sun 4-9:30
Closed major holidays   Wine and beer
Reservations not accepted   Street and lot parking
All major credit cards   Low to moderate

For bargain hunters who like huge portions and home-style Italian cooking, try this family restaurant. The pizza is great. For entrées, try seafood pastsa, shrimp scampi over linguine, or eggplant parmigiana. Complete menu to go.

World Famous   Steak & Seafood
711 Pacific Beach Drive (Pacific Beach)
San Diego 92109   272-3100

M-F 7-11, 11-3, 5-11; Sat-Sun 7-3, 4-11   Full bar
Open all holidays   Street parking (validate for Promenade)
Reservations recommended for 6 or more
All major credit cards   Low to expensive

Located on the boardwalk with an unobstructed ocean view, this fish and steak house is unpretentious and pleasant. Preparations are straightforward; the food is fresh; portions are large. Stay with fresh fish served with soup or salad and choice of rice, pasta, or potatoes. Or try combination plates with steak and seafood. Good brunch.

Smart Dining
in
La Jolla

Golden Triangle
La Jolla
La Jolla Shores

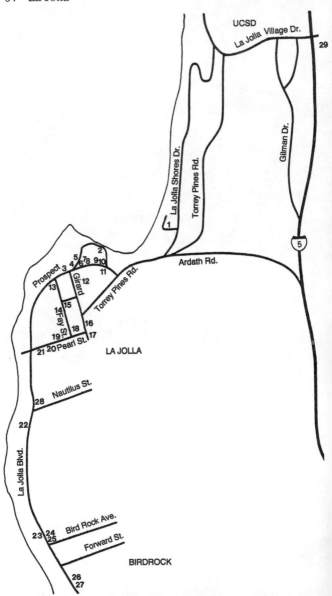

Open hours, menus, and prices change without notice. *Always call first.*

Map not exactly to scale.

Café Japengo   Pacific Rim
8960 University Center Lane, Aventine complex
San Diego 92122   450-3355

M-Th 11:30-2:30, 5:30-10; F 11-2:30, 5:30-11; Sat 5:30-11; Sun
    5:30-10; Sushi Bar: M-Th 5-11; F-Sat 5:30-12; Sun 5-10:30
Open all holidays   Full bar
Reservations accepted for dining room   Valet, street, & garage
All major credit cards   Moderate to expensive

No one does Pacific Rim better. You'll find recipes from China,
Japan, Thailand, Hawaii, and California done with verve and
originality. Menus change seasonally. Elegant and exciting.

Signature Dishes: Appetizers: grilled teriyaki chicken skewers;
sake shrimp; ahi layered with won tons. Entrées: roasted duck
with crispy vegetables; shrimp and scallops over spicy noodles;
fried rice with 10 ingredients. The sushi bar is one of the city's
best. **Dining Tip:** If you're on a budget, make a meal from one
or two appetizers. When ordering sushi, note prices or your bill
will be larger than expected. Live music M night.

George's at the Cove   Creative California region
1250 Prospect Street
La Jolla 92037   454-4244

M-Th 11:30-2:30, 5:30-10; F 11:30-2:30, 5-11; Sat 5-11; Sun
    11:30-3, 5:30-10
Closed Christmas Day, open Christmas night   Full bar
Reservations accepted   Valet parking
AE, MC, V   Expensive

California cuisine with emphasis on fish and seafood is
consistently high quality. Ocean view and three dining rooms.
George's is a few steps down.

Signature Dishes: Appetizers: Soup made with smoked chicken,
black beans, and broccoli; rock shrimp fettucine. Entrées: White
fish with potato crust; charbroiled smoked salmon with fennel;
Maine scallops on bed of corn and tortilla strips; rack of lamb;
ravioli stuffed with Gorgonzola and walnuts. **Dining Tip:**
Wonderful spot to entertain visitors at lunch.

George's at the Cove, The Terrace   California
1250 Prospect Street, La Jolla 92037   454-4244

Sun-Th 11-10; F-Sat 11-11
Open all holidays (closed only if it rains)   Full bar
Reservations not accepted   Valet parking
AE, MC, V   Low to moderate

The Terrace, with ocean view, no ceiling, is a flight up (or take elevator at side of building). Offers 20 items, opening to closing.
Signature Dishes: Ginger marinated chicken; tortellini; mahi mahi; soups and salads. **Dining Tip:** Try Sun brunch/lunch with 16 items for $9 or less.

Maitre D'   Continental
5523 La Jolla Boulevard, La Jolla 92037   456-2111

Tu-Sat 6 pm-11 pm
Closed Christmas, New Years Day   Full bar
Reservations required   Free parking
All major credit cards   Expensive

Elegant ambiance and faultless service contribute to a fine dining experience. Champagne glasses are Lalique, and sorbet is served in lighted, frozen swans.
Signature Dishes: Half lobster appetizer, rack of lamb, fresh fish daily. In season, order the flown-in sturgeon. **Dining Tip:** Reservations are a must. Russian Festival in late Oct and Nov. Gypsy violinist included with meal.

Manhattan of La Jolla   Northern Italian
7766 Fay Ave. (Empress Hotel), LJ 92037   554-1444

M-F 11:30-2, 5-10:30; Sat-Sun 5-10:30
Closed July 4, Thanksgiving, Christmas, New Year's Day   Full bar
Reservations necessary for dinner   Valet parking
All major credit cards   Moderate to expensive

Long for New York-style Italian? Then enjoy the first-rate food, high energy, and sporting crowd here. Best steaks in the city.
Signature Dishes: Cannelloni; pasta with fresh, lightly-coated tomatoes; Mediterranean seafood stew; steaks; rack of lamb. Inquire about nightly fresh fish. **Dining Tip:** Lunch is low cost.

Sky Room, La Valencia Hotel
1132 Prospect Street, La Jolla 92037

French
454-0771

M-Sat 6 pm-9 pm
Open all holidays
Reservations necessary
All major credit cards

Full bar
Valet parking
Expensive

Located on the 10th floor, this gourmet dining room offers a sweeping view of the coast and an elegant atmosphere.

Signature Dishes: Â la carte: Fresh fish, shrimp, lobster, and scallops in bouillabaisse sauce; filet mignon. Fixed price meals are in the $40-$50 range. **Dining Tip:** Have an appetizer and wine for low budget. Very romantic.

Triangles Restaurant
4370 La Jolla Village Drive, La Jolla 92037

American low-fat, low-cal
453-6650

M-F 11:30-2, 5:30-10; Sat-Sun 5:30-10
Closed Christmas, New Year's Day
Reservations accepted
All major credit cards

Full bar
Free garage parking
Moderate to upper moderate

Many low-cal, low-fat dishes are available here. Beautiful patio.

Signature Dishes: Breast of free range chicken; baked crab cakes with lobster sauce; lemon linguine with Tiger shrimp; meat loaf with mashed potatoes.

Tutto Mare
4365 Executive Dr., Hahn Towers, LJ 92037

Italian fish/seafood
597-1188

M-F 11:30-11; Sat 5-12; Sun 5-10
Closed major holidays
Reservations accepted
Major credit cards (not Discover)

Full bar
Valet or self parking
Moderate to expensive

The name means "everything from the sea," but chicken and meat are available as well.

Signature Dishes: Salmon medallions; mixed seafood with vegetables; grilled sea scallops with roasted peppers; Dover sole; *cioppino* (Italian tomato-based seafood soup); lamb with black olive sauce; fettucine with sweet water prawns. Easter and Passover dinners are a must.

Aesop's Tables
Greek and Mediterranean
8650 Genesee Avenue, Costa Verde Shopping Cntr., #106
(Golden Triangle) San Diego 92122   455-1535

M 11-9; Tu-Sat 11-10; Sun 4-9
Closed major holidays   Full bar
Reservations for 5 or more   Underground parking
All major credit cards   Low to low moderate

The chief attributes of this Greek and Mediterranean restaurant
are fresh food, tasty preparations, low costs. You may have
dinner for $10 or less. Salads are memorable; entrées are large
enough for two. The pitza—hot pita bread with a variety of
toppings—is especially noteworthy, as are the Moroccan-style
chicken pie and the white fish when available.

Alfonso's of La Jolla
Jalisco Mexican
1251 Prospect St., La Jolla 92037   454-2232

M-Th 11-11; F-Sat 11 am-12 midnight; Sun 11-10   Full bar
Closed Thanksgiving, Christmas Eve, Christmas holidays
Reservations accepted for 6 or more   Valet or street parking
All major credit cards   Low to moderate

Lively, crowded, noisy, and festive. The specialty is carne asada,
but the steak picado (beef sautéed with Mexican sausage), the
Guadalajara-style baked chicken (available on F and Sat nights),
and shrimp Mercedes (shrimp over quesadilla) are outstanding.
Fabulous strawberry sopapilla dessert. Outdoor patio.

Avalon
American
6941 La Jolla Blvd., La Jolla 92037   456-2535

Daily 10:30-2:30, 5-9
Open all major holidays   Full bar
Reservations accepted   Free parking in back
All major credit cards   Low to moderate

You'll get your money's worth here for fresh fish, prime rib, and
seafood. Call to find out which dinner or entrée is the low-cost
special. Sun and M, a four-course meal is available for $12.95.

Avanti Italian Restaurant
Northern Italian

875 Prospect St., La Jolla 92037   454-4288

Sun-Th 5-11; F-Sat 5-2 am
Closed Christmas   Full bar
Reservations recommended   Free underground parking
Major credit cards (not Discover)   Moderate

The Northern Italian food, contemporary decor, and attentive service won't disappoint you. Try the early bird four-course dinner served 5:30-7 daily for $12.95. Another option is dinner for two for $19.95, with appetizer, salad, entrée, and dessert. It's available all night, Sun-Th; F and Sat to 7 pm. Piano playing nightly, dancing Tu-Sat, opera singers some Sundays. Good food and good fun.

Baked by Etta
Bakery and Coffeehouse

7523 Fay Avenue (Vons Mall), La Jolla 92037   551-8107

M-F 7-6; Sat 7-5; Sun 7-3
Closed Christmas   No alcohol
Reservations not accepted   Parking in lot
No credit cards   Low

"Just like mother used to bake—only better" would perfectly describe the lemon poppy seed cake and the chocolate chip coffee cake. In summer try the fresh fruit, virtually sugarless pies. Flourless chocolate cake is fabulous. Many nonfat treats are available. Have dessert on the premises with gourmet tea or coffee, or take out.

Bonfires
Italian

8008 Girard Avenue, La Jolla 92037   551-8200

M-F 11-11; Sat-Sun 8-11
Open all holidays   Full bar
Reservations accepted   Street parking
All major credit cards   Low

For lunch and dinner, Bonfires offers wood-fired pizzas as well as salads and pasta. Pasta and pizza specials available nightly. Casual atmosphere; attentive service. One flight up or take the elevator at left of the building.

Chang Cuisine of China Mandarin & Szechuan
8670 Genesee Ave., Costa Verde Center Chinese
(Golden Triangle) San Diego 92122 558-2288

M-Th 11:30-10; F 11:30-11; Sat 12-11; Sun 12-10
Open all holidays Full bar
Reservations accepted Parking in front
All major credit cards Low to moderate

The palatial setting and beautiful art carry this restaurant. Food is of average competence. Best dishes are crispy beef, minced chicken in lettuce cups, and honey chicken. Low-calorie/low-fat menu on request. Dinner available opening to closing Sat and Sun.

Cindy Black's French Provincial
5721 La Jolla Blvd., La Jolla 92037 456-6299

M-Th 5:30-10; F 11:30-2, 5:30-10; Sat 5:30-10; Sun 5-8
Closed Memorial Day Full bar
Reservations accepted Street or parking; complimentary valet F, Sat
All major credit cards Moderate to expensive

Cindy Black's French provincial entrées are fresh, innovative, and good value. Best bet is Sunday night dinner. served 5-8 pm. It includes soup or salad, entrée, and dessert for $15.95. Friday lunch is also fine value for $12.95. Menus change seasonally. When available, select the Norwegian salmon or duck with ginger and leeks. Interesting room, good service.

Daily's Low-fat/Low-calorie
8915 Towne Centre Dr., (Golden Tri.) 92122 453-1112

M-Sat 10:30-9; Sun 11-8
Closed Thanksgiving, Christmas No alcohol
Reservations not accepted Parking in front of mall
No credit cards Low

Owned by a doctor, this restaurant offers a low-fat, low-calorie, low-sodium menu. All the dishes look and taste wonderful, and the top price is $6.95. Sandwiches and salads are first-rate, and the leaf spinach and curly pasta or the Chinatown chicken salad are especially good. Also to be commended: chili with three beans, and corn with brown rice. Many vegetarian dishes.

Harry's Café Gallery
American
7545 Girard Avenue, La Jolla 92037
454-7381

M-Sat 5:30 am-2:30 pm; Sun 5:30 am-2 pm
Closed major holidays   No alcohol
Reservations accepted for 8 or more   Free parking in rear lot
All major credit cards   Low

This landmark restaurant is noted for its breakfasts, served all day. The buttermilk pancakes, waffles made from scratch, and egg combinations are all generous and well prepared. Harry's serves hot oatmeal or cream of wheat, freshly squeezed orange juice and entire carafes of freshly ground coffee.

HOPS! Bistro and Brewery
International
4353 La Jolla Village Drive (north of the Broadway in University Towne Centre), San Diego 92122   587-6677

Sun-Th 11:30-8; F-Sat 11:30-10
Closed major holidays   Beer brewed on premises
Reservations accepted   Free parking in mall lot
All major credit cards   Low to moderate

HOPS! serves the best food of any brewery in San Diego. Best dishes are spit-roasted chicken; penne with salmon and shrimp; Thai beef salad; spicy linguine; cracked rye-pumpernickel Reuben. All beers brewed on premises; try the raspberry lager.

Khatoon Persian Cuisine
Persian
639 Pearl St., La Jolla 92037
459-4016

M-Th 11:30-9; F-Sun 11-10
Open all holidays   Wine and beer
Reservations preferred   Parking in front
All major credit cards   Low to moderate

Persian cuisine is very healthy nonfat or low-fat—and this menu consists mostly of meat, fish, and skinless chicken kabobs served with basmati rice and broiled tomatoes. Lamb shanks (boiled) are available Sat and Sun but sell out quickly. Best bets are the chicken kabobs or the ground beef and filet combinations. Same menu all day; dinner portions larger. Good-tasting fresh food, but not too exotic.

La Jolla Spice Co. American; French (at dinner only)
5737 La Jolla Blvd., La Jolla 92037   456-2272

Nightly 7:30 pm-10 pm
Call about holidays   Wine and beer
Reservations accepted   Parking in the front/side
All major credit cards   Low to upper moderate

If you've been searching for Chef Pierre Lustrat, formerly of L'Escargot, he can be found every night preparing light French meals at this café. The setting is quite charming and among the best bets are the fresh fish dinners, which change nightly and include soup or salad. The bouillabaisse and wiener schnitzel are also delightful. Best of all is Pierre's famous Tarte Tatin dessert; please call an hour in advance to order it.

La Terrazza   Italian
8008 Girard Avenue, La Jolla 92037   459-9750

Daily 11:30-11
Closed first 3 weeks in December   Wine and beer
Reservations accepted   Street or underground parking
All major credit cards   Low to moderate

A pleasant Italian café with festive atmosphere. Best are pastas and salads. A good place for casual dining. Same menu lunch and dinner except for specials.

The Mediterranean Room   Continental/American
La Valencia Hotel, 1132 Prospect Street
La Jolla 92037   454-0771

M-Sat 11:30-2:30, 5-8 (F-Sat till 9); Sun 11:30-2:30, 4:30-8
Open all holidays   Full bar
Reservations accepted   Free valet parking
AE, MC, V   Moderate to expensive

Noted for its excellent Sunday brunch, this lovely view-room also offers fixed price "sundowner" dinners ($14.25-$15.50) M-Sat, 5-7:30 pm, with plain, home-style entrées like fish, short ribs, and small steaks. Call for brunch 24 hours in advance. The view, setting, and food are worth the effort.

Milagro Bean Company
California Cuisine

4150 Regents Park Row (Golden Triangle)
San Diego 92122   450-2128

M-F 6:30 am-11 pm; Sat 7:30 am-11 pm; Sun 7:30 am-4:30
Closed Thanksgiving, Christmas   Wine and beer
Reservations not accepted   Parking in lot
MC, V   Low

While the menu is basically California cuisine, Italian items
(especially pasta) are best sellers. Try angel hair pasta and the
penne tossed with fresh salmon. If dinner for two for $14.95 is
available, don't hesitate to order it.

Milligan's Bar and Grill
American

5786 La Jolla Boulevard, La Jolla 92037   459-7311

Daily 11:30-2:30, 5-10:30
Closed Christmas   Full bar
Reservations accepted   Free parking lot
All major credit cards   Moderate

Complete fried chicken dinners at $9.95 on Th and Sun. Ribs,
fresh fish, mashed potatoes. Good food; friendly atmosphere.
Excellent Happy Hour. View from upstairs.

Ocean Kitchen
Mandarin & Cantonese Chinese

5525 La Jolla Blvd., La Jolla 92037   459-3993

M-Th 11:30-9:30; F-Sat 11:30-10:30; Sun 4:30-9:30
Closed Thanksgiving, Christmas   Wine and beer
Reservations accepted   Street parking
AE, MC, V   Low to moderate

Mandarin and Cantonese preparations using no MSG in the food
nor starches in the sauces. Try the shrimp toast for appetizer and
the crispy shrimp served with their shells. Shaw San Tung, a
vegetable dish with black mushrooms, is outstanding as are the
shrimp in black bean sauce and the chicken dishes.

Panda Country   Chinese
4150 Regents Park Row, #190, University Towne Center
San Diego 92122   552-1345

M-F 11-10; Sat-Sun 12-10
Closed Thanksgiving   Full bar
Reservations accepted   Underground parking
All major credit cards   Low to expensive

Gorgeous surroundings and stunning presentations define this restaurant. Particularly well prepared are the 13 appetizers and the 28 seafood and fish dishes Mandarin- or Szechuan-style. Scallops and shrimp receive special treatment. Though it's somewhat pricey, you won't be disappointed here.

The Pannikin Café   Coffeehouse
7467 Girard Avenue, La Jolla 92037   454-5453

M-Th 6 am-10 pm; F 6 am-11 pm; Sat-Sun 7 am-11 pm
Call about holidays   No alcohol
Reservations not accepted   Street parking
All major credit cards   Low expensive

The outdoor seating area is almost always crowded with tea and coffee drinkers sunning themselves, reading, or chatting. Light meals—pasta, soup, salads, quiche—are served till 4 pm; tea, coffee, and pastries thereafter. Different hours for summer and winter.

Pannikin's Brockton Villa   Coffeehouse
1235 Coast Boulevard, La Jolla 92037   454-7393

M-Tu 8-5; W-Sun 8 am-10 pm
Call about holidays   Wine and beer
Dinner reservations for 8 or more   Street parking
All major credit cards   Snacks, lunch—low; dinner—low to moderate

A coffeehouse and restaurant, it's worth visiting just to experience one of the oldest beach houses in La Jolla. Outdoor dining is available on several levels. Best for breakfast, or beverages plus pastries. Different hours for summer and winter.

Piatti Ristorante
California-style Italian
2182 Avenida de la Playa (LJ Shores) 92037   454-1589

M-F 11:30-3, 5-10; Sat-Sun 11-3, 5-11
Open all holidays   Full bar
Reservations recommended   Street parking
AE,, MC, V   Moderate

Piatti is a country-style restaurant serving admirable Italian dishes with light sauces. Not to be missed are the daily soups, rotisserie chicken with roasted potatoes, vegetarian lasagne, ravioli in lemon sauce. Sat and Sun à la carte brunch offers 14 outstanding items including eggs benedict, strawberry pancakes, sweet calzone, omelets, and pizza. A treasure.

Rusty Pelican
Fish/seafood
4340 La Jolla Village Drive (Golden Triangle)
San Diego 92122   587-1886

M-Th 11:30-4, 4-10; F 11:30-4, 4-11; Sat 4-11; Sun 4-10
Call about holidays   Full bar
Reservations accepted   Valet parking during the day and on F night
All major credit cards   Low to upper moderate

The fish and seafood are fresh and satisfying. Best bet is the sunset dinner served daily between 5 and 6:30 pm: salad or soup, fish with potato or rice, vegetables, bread, dessert, and beverage for $9.95. Try to get a table overlooking the lagoon.

Sadaf Restaurant
Persian
613 Pearl Street, La Jolla 92037   551-0643

Sun-Th 11:30-9:30; F-Sat 11:30-10:30
Open all holidays   Wine and beer
Reservations accepted   Free parking
All major credit cards   Low to moderate

The best Persian food in the city. Stuffed grape leaves and two styles of eggplant are noteworthy for appetizers. Choice entrées are chicken barg (flat strips) or chicken kabob and filet mignon strips. The most stunning preparations are rice dishes: dill with lima beans; currants with sweet carrots; buttery basmati. Mammoth portions. Order yogurt with entrées.

Sammy's Woodfired Pizza Restaurant
702 Pearl Street   California-style pizza & pasta
La Jolla 92037   456-5222

Sun-Th 11:30-10; F-Sat 11:30-11
Closed Thanksgiving, Christmas   Wine and beer
Reservations for 6 or more   Street parking
DC, MC, V   Low to low moderate

You have a choice of 20 wood-fired pizzas, most with exotic toppings. Among the best are barbecue chicken, New York-style (pepperoni, sausage, salami), and vegetarian (eggplant, mushroom). Many come here for the salads: Caesar, chopped salad, Thai chicken salad, or grilled breast of chicken with walnuts. Each is large enough for two. Half orders on some salads.

Sante Ristorante   Northern Italian
7811 Herschel Avenue, La Jolla 92037   454-1315

M-Th 11:30-3, 5-10:30; F 11:30-3, 5-11; Sat 5-11; Sun 5-10:30
Closed July 4, Christmas, New Year's Day   Full bar
Reservations accepted   Street parking
All major credit cards   Moderate to expensive

Although this Northern Italian restaurant is pricey, the room is soothing and the chopped salad and pasta dishes are outstanding. Tony Buonsante will prepare any pasta you like in any manner you prefer. Don't overlook broad white noodles with shiitake and sautéed mushrooms. Lunch is a best bet, especially with visitors.

Soup Exchange   Soup and Salad
7777 Fay Avenue, La Jolla 92037   459-0212

Daily 11-9
Closed Thanksgiving, Christmas   Wine and beer
Reservations not accepted   Underground parking
No credit cards   Low

Does La Jolla offer bargains? It does indeed at the Soup Exchange, an all-you-can-eat soup-and-salad bar, where the items (including pasta salads) are fresh, tasty, and inexpensive. Price includes muffins, pizza, baked potatoes, and dessert. Very attractive surroundings; charming dining patio.

Star of India
Indian
1000 Prospect Street, La Jolla 92037   459-3355

M-F 11:30-2:30, 5-10; Sat 12-3, 5-10:30; Sun 12-3, 5-10
Open all holidays	Wine and beer
Reservations accepted	Street parking
All major credit cards	Moderate to expensive

The Indian food is well prepared and the menu extensive. À la carte items are somewhat pricey, and there is a cost for bread. Best buy is the all-you-can-eat buffet lunch or the Sat and Sun champagne buffet brunch. Excellent vegetarian selections. Branches in Encinitas (927 First Street, 632-1113) and downtown (423 F Street, 544-9891).

Su Casa Restaurante
Mexican
6738 La Jolla Boulevard, La Jolla 92037   454-0369

M-Th 11:30-9:30; F-Sat 11:30-11; Sun 10-2, 4-10
Closed Thanksgiving evening, Christmas	Full bar
Reservations accepted	Parking in lot
All major credit cards	Low to moderate

Su Casa has returned to regional Mexican cooking, and the homemade corn tamale stuffed with crab and shrimp, the tacos, the shrimp fajitas, and the carnitas Michoacan are well prepared. All-you-can-eat Sun brunch $8.95. Indoor fireplace; patio dining.

The Whaling Bar
Fish/seafood
La Valencia Hotel, 1132 Prospect Street
La Jolla 92037   454-0771

Daily 11:30-4, 6-10 (F-Sat till 11)
Open all major holidays	Full bar
Reservations accepted	Free valet parking
Major credit cards (not Discover)	Moderate to expensive

The only non-view restaurant of the three located at the La Valencia Hotel, the Whaling Bar has a wide range of à la carte dishes for both lunch and dinner. The best, available for both meals, are fresh fish and a superb paella.

Smart Dining
in
North County

Carlsbad
Del Mar
Encinitas
Escondido
Lake Hodges
Miramar
Mira Mesa
Rancho Bernardo
Rancho Peñasquitos
Rancho Santa Fe
San Marcos
Scripps Ranch
Solana Beach
Vista

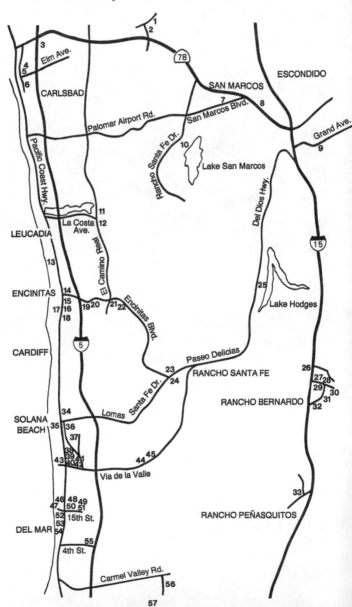

Open hours, menus, and prices change without notice. *Always call first.*

Map not exactly to scale.

Brasserie and WineSeller
French/California

9550 Waples Street, #115 (Mira Mesa)
San Diego 92121   450-9576

Tu-F 5:30-10; Sat 11:30-2, 6-10; Sun 5:30-9
Closed major holidays   Wine and beer
Reservations required   Free parking
All major credit cards   Moderate to expensive

Voted one of the best restaurants in the country, the Brasserie serves contemporary French/California cuisine that delights the eye and the palate. Exquisite. Call for driving directions.

Signature Dishes: Appetizers: Basil cured salmon; grilled lamb; duck salad. Entrées: Salmon with red beet vinaigrette; yellowfin tuna with fava beans; roasted chicken breast with zucchini ravioli; grilled lamb loin with black olive sauce. Desserts Hazelnut cannoli; flourless chocolate cake. **Dining Tip:** Sunday night three-course dinner for $17.95 is a winner. Or try lunch Saturday afternoon with wine tasting.

Chez Henri
French provincial

1555 Camino Del Mar (Del Mar Plaza, market level)
Del Mar 92014   793-0067

M-Sat 11:30-2:30, 5:30-10; Sun 5:30-10   Wine and beer
Closed Christmas, New Year's Day; call about Thanksgiving
Reservations accepted   Validated parking
All major credit cards   Moderate to expensive

Those accustomed to traditional French provincial food frequent this dining room (on entrance level) supervised by chef/owner Henri.

Signature Dishes: Whole fish (prepared for two or more) cooked under a blanket of sea salt which is then removed; filet mignon, with or without goose liver; Tuesday night, thrilling cassoulet of white beans, fresh duck, lamb chop, and imported sausage; Thursday night, bouillabaisse (fish in saffron); Sunday-Thursday, fixed price meal (soup, salad, choice of two entrées, dessert), $16.50. **Dining Tip:** For budget dining try one of the excellent soups plus salad or the low-cost *coq au vin* (chicken in wine sauce).

Epazote's

Southwestern

1555 Camino Del Mar (Del Mar Plaza)
Del Mar 92014   259-9966

M-Th 11:30-10; F-Sat 11:30-11; Sun 11-9:30   Full bar
Closed Thanksgiving, Christmas; open till 6 pm Christmas Eve
Reservations recommended   Validated parking
AE, MC, V   Low to expensive

The restaurant boasts a covered outdoor patio but inside is where the action is.

Signature Dishes: Chile-rubbed, free-range spit-roasted chicken; grilled vegetable platter; charbroiled Atlantic salmon; shrimp chile relleno; and grilled ahi. Or make a meal from appetizers such as tamales; vegetable tostada; Jamaican blackened fish taco. **Dining Tip:** À la carte Sun brunch offers eggs Benedict; roasted pepper omelet; carne asada with eggs; plus mimosa (champagne and orange juice). Intense and noisy weekends.

Mille Fleurs

Nouvelle French cuisine

6009 Paseo Delicias
Rancho Santa Fe 92067   756-3085

M-F 11:30-2:30, 6-10; Sat 5:30-10; Sun 6-10
Closed Christmas, New Year's Day   Full bar
Reservations highly recommended   Street parking
Major credit cards (not Discover)   Expensive

Every year brings fresh awards and prizes to this outstanding restaurant. Menus change nightly and the host-owner adds special cachet to the proceedings. Count on $65 per person for dinner.

Signature Dishes: Appetizers: Beef, salmon, or lamb tartare (raw chopped ingredients plus capers and onions); boned trout with salmon mousse; or any incredible soup. Entrées when available: Breaded lotte (fish from north Pacific); white sea bass in black olive crust; Dover sole; salmon and halibut in rice paper; lamb with lentils. **Dining Tip:** If you can't quite afford Mille Fleurs, order the least expensive entrée and no wine, then call it a night. An appetizer and soup cost almost as much as a low-end entrée.

Overseas Restaurant
2818 Roosevelt Street
Carlsbad 92008

Hong Kong/Singapore
Chinese
729-0348

Sun-Th 11:30-9; F-Sat 11:30-10
Closed Easter, July 4, Thanksgiving, Christmas
Reservations accepted
All major credit cards

Wine and beer
Parking in front
Moderate

It's worth driving here for Hong Kong and Singapore as well as Mandarin and Szechuan dishes.

Signature Dishes: Overseas Supreme (chicken, shrimp, beef, and cashews in a ring of deep-fried mashed potatoes) and shark's fin with lettuce cups. Excellent shrimp dishes. Gorgeous presentation includes carved vegetables. **Dining Tip:** Some of the best dishes appear on a separate menu written in Chinese. Ask Kenny, the owner, to translate and order a few of them.

Pacifica Del Mar
Del Mar Plaza, 1555 Pacific Coast Highway
Del Mar 92014

American

792-0476

M-Th 11-10; F-Sat 11-10:30; Sun 9 am-10 pm; open till 11 pm
    during racing season
Open all holidays
Reservations accepted
All major credit cards

Full bar
Underground validated parking
Low moderate to expensive

The wonderful view, the fresh fish, and the excellent pastas make this restaurant a good choice for lunch or dinner. The light sunset dinners, served 4-6:30 pm, offer pasta, salads, entrées, and sandwiches.

Signature Dishes: Chicken pappardelle (braised chicken with spinach and artichokes over broad noodles); Alaskan halibut with potato cakes; Hawaiian swordfish with King crab legs; barbecued King salmon; or mustard chicken with mashed potatoes. **Dining Tip:** A great favorite for visitors because of the view and fresh fish.

Panevino Gastronomia
Tuscan Italian

3050 Pio Pico Drive (off Carlsbad Village Drive)
Carlsbad 92008   720-3377

M-Th 11:30-2:30, 5-10:30; F 11:30-2:30, 5:30-11:30; Sat 5:30-11:30;
    Sun 5-10:30
Call about holidays   Full bar
Reservations accepted   Free valet parking
All major credit cards   Moderate to expensive

A sister restaurant to Panevino downtown. This is more family-oriented with two dining rooms upstairs and a full pizzeria downstairs. Classy open kitchen.

Signature Dishes: Daily ravioli and gnocchi; excellent risotta; shrimp with lentils and white beans; fresh fish. The pastas are in a class of their own. **Dining Tip:** Don't expect the intimacy of downtown, but do bring children and grandparents.

Tourlas L'Auberge
California-French

Del Mar Hotel, 1540 Camino del Mar
Del Mar 92014   259-1515

Daily 6:30 am-10 pm
Open all holidays   Full bar
Reservations accepted   Valet and validated self parking
All major credit cards   Moderate to expensive

The new chef has completely revamped the menu, which offers California specialties with French influence. Romantic surroundings indoors as well as on the patio.

Signature Dishes: Baked salmon; baked halibut with shrimp and scallop sauce; tenderloin of beef in wine/truffle sauce; rack of lamb with white bean cassoulet; chicken stuffed with goat cheese and sun dried tomatoes. **Dining Tip:** Try the all-you-can-eat Sunday buffet brunch with fresh seafood bar (shrimp, oysters, sushi, smoked salmon); omelet and waffle stations; carving station; breakfast and lunch items.

When in Rome
Italian

1108 First Street
Encinitas 92024

944-1771

Tu-F 11:30-2:30; Sat 5:30-10; Sun 5-9; open daily during racing
  season
Closed Easter, Christmas   Full bar
Reservations recommended   Parking front and back; valet weekends
AE, MC, V   Moderate to expensive

This is a glorious restaurant featuring specialties from Rome. The
18 pastas are prepared from scratch as are the bread and desserts.
Very fastidious preparations, superb service, attractive
surroundings. Don't miss this one.

Signature Dishes: Risotto; combination plate of three pastas
(lasagne, ravioli, fusilli with vodka); chicken with artichokes;
grilled lamb chops; stuffed salmon; swordfish topped with
seafood; Dover sole; pear tart; tiramisu. **Dining Tip:** If you are
on a budget, order the three pasta combination plate. Each pasta
is distinctive and memorable.

Anthony's Rancho Bernardo
Fish/seafood

11666 Avena Place (off Bernardo Center Drive)
Rancho Bernardo 92128

451-2070

Daily 11:30-8:30
Closed major holidays   Full bar
Reservations accepted   Free parking in lot
AE, MC, V   Low to low moderate

A handsome branch of Anthony's, this restaurant accepts
reservations for parties of five or more. Less frantic than the
downtown branches. Good fish and chips, seafood salads,
broiled fish. Fast service.

The Armenian Café
Armenian
3126 Carlsbad Boulevard, Carlsbad 92008   720-2233

W-F 11-3, 5-9; Sat-Sun 8-9; Belly dancing F, Sat nights
Open all major holidays	Wine and beer
Reservations accepted for 6 or more	Free parking in lot
All major credit cards	Low to moderate

New items include rack of lamb for dinner and various combination plates. Try *potlejan* (eggplant, beef, and potatoes topped with cheese) and the prepared-on-the-premises gyros. Soups and desserts are terrific. Unique breakfasts include omelets filled with chicken or lamb kabobs served Sat and Sun, 8 am-1:30 pm.

Ashoka the Great
Indian
9474 Black Mountain Road (off Miramar Road)
San Diego 92126   695-9749

Daily 11:30-3:15, 5-10
Open all holidays	Wine and beer
Reservations accepted	Parking in lot
MC, V	Low to moderate

One of our best Indian restaurants, Ashoka offers a lovely setting, excellent service, and first-rate food. Don't overlook the tandoori dishes or the lamb stew. Ten vegetable platters and six rice dishes for vegetarians. An all-you-can-eat lunch buffet is served daily—one of the few good ones in San Diego. It's not difficult to find if you obtain directions.

Baja Grill and Fish Market
Fish/seafood
1342 Camino Del Mar, Del Mar 92014   792-6472

M-F 11:30-9:30; Sat-Sun 9 am-10 pm
Closed Thanksgiving, Christmas	Full bar
Reservations accepted for 6 or more	Parking in rear
All major credit cards	Low

Casual beach atmosphere; but the menu offers a good fish taco platter, shrimp and crab quesadilla, seafood relleno, and charbroiled chicken tacos. Breakfasts Sat and Sun only include banana pancakes, Baja scrambled eggs, and omelets.

Beach Hut Café
American

106 South Sierra, Solana Beach 92075   794-9536

Daily 7-4
Closed Thanksgiving, Christmas, New Year's Day   No alcohol
Reservations not accepted   Parking in front
No credit cards   Low

A gorgeous outdoor patio (with retractable cover during winter)
and an unobstructed ocean view make this casual restaurant a
good place for breakfast, lunch, and light items. Omelets, salads,
great sandwiches, smoothies, coffees, and teas.

Bernard O's
French, California

Rancho Bernardo Village , 12457 Rancho Bernardo Road
Rancho Bernardo 92128   487-7171

Tu-F 11:30-2, 5:30-9; Sat 11:30-2, 5:30-9:30, Sun 5:30-8:30
Closed major holidays   Wine and beer
Reservations accepted   Parking in front
All major credit cards   Moderate to expensive

This charming French-Californian café serves exquisite food.
Make a meal from French onion soup plus spinach salad and a
potato pancake; or from pasta or gourmet pizza. As an entrée,
select when available sautéed chicken breast in lime butter;
grilled salmon in Dijon mustard sauce; filet mignon; lamb
medallions; duck breast in orange ginger glaze; crêpe with fresh
pear. Menu changes seasonally. Fixed price meals for holidays.

The Brasserie, La Costa Resort
Continental, American

Costa Del Mar Rd. (off El Camino Real)
Carlsbad 92009   438-9111, ext. 4500

Sun-Th 6:30 am-10 pm; F-Sat 6:30 am-11 pm
Open major holidays   Full bar
Reservations accepted   Validated parking
All major credit cards   Expensive

One of the few all-you-can-eat fish and seafood buffets, this
dining room offers shrimp, crab, clams, mussels, fish, and
smoked salmon. Available Friday night only, $32.50. Continental
and American dinners are served other nights of the week.

Bully's North
American beef

1404 Camino del Mar, Del Mar 92014 755-1660

Daily 10:30-4, 4:30-12; extended hours during racing season
Closed Thanksgiving, Christmas | Full bar
Reservations not accepted | Parking on side
Major credit cards (not Discover) | Low to moderate

Especially in summer, this branch is jammed with the sporting crowd, which makes the place colorful and exciting. Steak and prime rib are favorites. Good-quality hamburgers and fries remain a best bet. Breakfast items available to 4 pm include steak and egg and killer omelets.

Cajun Connection
Cajun/New Orleans

740 Nordahl Road (off Highway 78)
San Marcos 92069 741-5680

Tu-F 11:30-9:30; Sat 4-9:30; Sun 4-9
Closed major holidays | Wine and beer
Reservations accepted for 6 or more | Parking in front
All major credit cards | Moderate

This unpretentious New Orleans-style restaurant serves crawfish étouffée, jambalaya, and shrimp Creole on weekends, and other New Orleans dishes during week. Good bread pudding.

California Pizza Kitchen
California

437 South Highway 101, Suite 601
Solana Beach 92075 793-0999
La Jolla branch: 1044 Wall Street 551-9677
Carmel Mountain Ranch branch:
   11602 Carmel Mountain Road 675-4424

Sun-Th 11:30-10; F-Sat 11:30-11
Closed Thanksgiving, Christmas | Wine, beer, some mixed drinks
Reservations not accepted | Free parking; valet parking at LJ branch
All major credit cards | Low

Here's a good family restaurant for salads, pastas, and pizzas. Choose from 28 individual-size pizzas. Popular favorites are barbecue chicken and Thai chicken. Other memorable dishes are chicken tequila over spinach fettucine; Oriental chicken salad.

Canyon Grill
Southwestern, American
9823 Carroll Canyon Road (Scripps Ranch)
San Diego 92131 271-4052

M 11:30-2:30; Tu-Sat 11-9
Closed major holidays Full bar
Reservations accepted Parking in front
All major credit cards Low to upper moderate

The attractive setting includes a glassed-in patio that's open to
the sky and a Southwestern interior. Try the shrimp in achiote
sauce, penne with salmon, and any of the fresh grilled fish
entrées. The "kick-ass ribs" are popular, as are the focaccia
pizzas. Loving owners and staff. Great place for lunch.

Chung King Loh
Hong Kong Chinese
552 Stevens Avenue, Solana Beach 92075 481-0184

M-Th 11-9:30; F 11-10; Sat 12-10; Sun 4:30-9:30 Full bar
Closed Thanksgiving, Christmas Parking in front or back
Reservations not necessary except for large parties
All major credit cards Moderate to expensive

Hong Kong food at its best is served here. Try the onion
pancakes, lobster in black bean sauce, lemon chicken, and any
mu-shu dish. Extensive vegetarian menu. Art-filled interior.

Cilantro's Restaurant and Marketplace
Southwestern
3702 Via de la Valle, Del Mar 92014 259-8777

M-Sat 11:30-2:30, 5-10 (F-Sat till 10:30); Sun 11:30-2:30 (brunch),
5-9:30
Closed Thanksgiving, Christmas Full bar
Reservations recommended Valet parking
AE, MC, V Low to expensive

Love Southwestern cooking with robust flavor? Cilantro's serves
chile-rubbed salmon; lamb chops with salsa; grilled carne asada;
spit-roasted duck with tamales; free-range chicken with roasted
garlic. For a small meal, order tortilla soup and chicken Caesar
salad, chile-spiked chicken skewers or quesadilla with jalapeño
relish. Good service. Take-outs.

Dante's
Italian, Continental

9379 Mira Mesa Boulevard (Mira Mesa)
San Diego 92126   693-3252

M-Th 11:30-3, 4-9:30; F 11:30-3, 5-10; Sat 5-10
Closed major holidays   Full bar
Reservations accepted   Parking in front
AE, MC, V   Moderate to expensive

Well-prepared Italian and Continental dinners include soup or
salad, entrée, vegetables, pasta, or rice. Best buys are the
outstanding early bird dinners, served Monday-Thursday, 5-7
pm: soup or salad, choice of 10 entrées plus vegetables, pasta, or
potato for $8.95. Piano on weekends and lively atmosphere.

D. B. Hackers Seafood Café
Fish/seafood,

101 Highway 101   & pasta
Encinitas 92024   436-3162

M-Sat 11-9; Sun 12-8
Closed Easter, Christmas   Wine and beer
Reservations not necessary   Parking outside
AE, MC, V   Low

The dining room isn't impressive, but the all-you-can-eat fish
and chips served Monday-Thursday for $6.99 are terrific. The
fish (New Zealand hake) arrives in a golden crust that is well
drained and delicious. Smaller portions are available, or try the
"Kiddie" serving. Fresh fish and daily pastas are also
worthwhile.

Delicias
California/Continental

6106 Pasea Delicias, Rancho Santa Fe 92067   756-8000

Tu-Th 11-2, 6-10; F-Sat 11-2, 6-12 (possibly); Sun 11-2, 6-10
Closed Christmas, New Year's Day   Full bar
Reservations recommended   Free parking in front
All major credit cards   Expensive

Stylish, elegant dining room. Best bets: Dover sole; soft-shell
crab over linguine; fettucine with wild mushrooms and
asparagus; blackened tuna; filet mignon. Nightly specials are
notable.

Del Mar Pizza
211 15th Street, Del Mar 92014

Pizza
481-8088

Sun-Th 11:30-9; F-Sat 11:30-10
Closed Thanksgiving, Christmas
Reservations not accepted
No credit cards

Wine and beer
Free parking in rear
Low to moderate

If you've heard about New York pizza, the best is now in Del Mar. The hot sandwiches are good, but the pizza is in a league by itself. The secret lies in the crust. Lasagne, stuffed eggplant, and cannoli dessert are also available.

Di Crescenzo's
Westwood Shopping Center, 11625 Duenda Road
Rancho Bernardo 92128

Italian deli

487-2276

M-Sat 11:30-8:30
Closed July 4, Christmas
Reservations not needed
No credit cards

No alcohol
Parking in mall lot
Low

Italian sandwiches at their most seductive are prepared here, as well as pizza and light pasta dishes. The Italian beef and Rocco's Imperial sandwich with salami, ham, bologna, and cheese are both memorable. All items available for take-out, and "super loaves" that serve 12-15 are prepared on request.

El Bizcocho, Rancho Bernardo Inn
17550 Bernardo Oaks Drive
Rancho Bernardo 92128

Continental
American
277-2146, 487-1611

Daily 11-3, 6-10; Sun brunch 10-2
Open all holidays
Reservations required
All major credit cards

Full bar
Self or valet parking
Expensive

Located on a golf course, this à la carte dining room produces gorgeous entrées from prime ingredients. Fresh fish, rack of lamb, or roast duck with Calvados (prepared for two and carved tableside) are invariably good choices. Save room for the hot chocolate soufflé. Beautiful dining room, outstanding wine list. All-you-can-eat buffet brunch on Sun.

The Encinitas Café
Breakfast

531 First Street, Encinitas 92024   632-0919

Daily 5:30 am-9 pm; open 5:30 am-2 pm July 4, Christmas Eve,
    Christmas; open all day other holidays

Open all holidays; note hours	Wine and beer
Reservations not accepted	Parking in front and back
No credit cards	Low

American breakfasts are served from opening to closing. The Encinitas Special offers oatmeal pancakes with honey and almonds, two eggs, and either bacon, sausage, or ham for about $5. Biscuits and gravy arrive with eggs. Children's menus. Lunch and light dinner also available. Fast, excellent service.

Fidel's Carlsbad
Mexican

3003 Carlsbad Boulevard, Carlsbad 92008   729-0903

Sun-Th 11:30-9:30; F-Sat 11:30-10:30

Closed Thanksgiving, Christmas	Full bar
Reservations accepted for 10 or more	Free parking
MC, V	Low to moderate

A sister restaurant to the venerable establishment in Del Mar. Star dishes are carnitas; quesadilla with chicken, beef, or pork; tostada suprema; and breast of chicken Milanese.

Fish House Vera Cruz
Fish/seafood

Old California Row Center, 360 Via Vera Cruz
San Marcos 92069   744-8000

M-Th 11-9; F-Sat 11-10; Sun 11-9

Open most holidays	Full bar
No reservations	Parking in front
All major credit cards	Moderate to expensive

The new building ready at this address in late September will please you. Fresh fish and seafood change daily. Preparation is simple but honest.

The Fish Market
Fish/seafood

640 Via de la Valle, Del Mar 92075

755-2277

Daily 11-9:30; 11-10:30 in summer
Closed Thanksgiving, Christmas
Reservations for 8 or more
All major credit cards

Full bar
Self or valet parking
Low to expensive

There's scarcely a lull here all day. The reasons? Low to low-moderate prices, fresh food, on-the-run service, and about a dozen fresh fish choices, each accompanied by sourdough bread, cole slaw or cottage cheese, and potatoes or rice. Fine value, but not a quiet place.

Il Fornaio Cucina Italiana
California Italian

1555 Camino Del Mar (Del Mar Plaza)
Del Mar 92014

755-8876

M-Th 11:30-10; F 11:30-11:30; Sat 11-11:30; Sun 10-11
Closed Thanksgiving, Christmas
Reservations accepted
AE, DC, MC, V

Full bar
Validated parking
Low to expensive

Il Fornaio has a stunning view, with gorgeous seating both indoors and outdoors. Grilled items are uneven, but the stuffed focaccia, angel hair pasta, soups, and salads are good. Crowded. Sun brunch à la carte 10 am-3 pm. Very popular spot.

The Fortune Cookie
Hong Kong/Taiwan Chinese

16425 Bernardo Center Drive
Rancho Bernardo 92128

451-8958

Sun-Th 11-10; F-Sat 11-11
Closed Thanksgiving
Reservations recommended
All major credit cards

Full bar
Parking in mall lot
Low to expensive

Chef Henry Yang is from a five-star Taiwan restaurant. His unique cooking is Chinese with French influences. The shrimp toast, sea bass in wine sauce, bean curd soup, chef's special chicken, *jin do* (sweet and sour) pork chops, and stir-fried shrimp are all outstanding. Ask for Mr. Charlie to order for large parties or for special dishes. Superb product.

150 Grand Café
California/French
150 West Grand Avenue, Escondido 92025   738-6868

Daily 11:30-9; call for changes in hours   Full bar
Closed Christmas Eve, Christmas; call about other holidays
Reservations recommended   Parking in rear lot
All major credit cards   Low to moderate

This beautifully decorated room (plus separate bar) offers California food with French influences. The top price for an entrée is $14. Soups and salads are à la carte. Tempting salads, pastas, and excellent dill rolls. Filet mignon in wine sauce is a best bet.

Hernandez' Hide-Away
Mexican
Rancho and Lake Drives, Lake Hodges 92025   746-1444

Tu-Th 3-9; F 3-10; Sat 10-10; Sun 10-9
Closed Thanksgiving, one week at Christmas   Full bar
Reservations accepted   Free parking
All major credit cards   Low to moderate

Noted for authentic Mexican cooking and large portions, this restaurant remains popular especially for its weekend breakfast/brunches that include steak and eggs, chilaquiles, sausage, beans, and omelets. Fine dinner entrées are chicken enchiladas with spicy sour cream, stuffed quesadillas, tamales, and chiles rellenos.

Jake's Del Mar
American/Seafood, steaks
1660 Coast Boulevard, Del Mar 92014   755-2002

Tu-Sat 11:15-2:30, 5-9:30 (F-Sat till 10); Sun 10-2:30, 5-9:30
Closed Thanksgiving, Christmas;   Full bar
    call about other holidays
Reservations recommended   Valet parking
AE, MC, V   Moderate to expensive

Jake's is high spirited "Southern California." Most tables offer an ocean view and everyone has a good time, which counts as much as the food. The best bet here is fresh fish accompanied by rice or pasta. À la carte Sunday brunch attracts young professionals.

Khayyam Cuisine Restaurant   Middle Eastern
437 Highway 101, Solana Beach 92075   755-6343

Tu-Sat 11:30-2:30, 5:30-10:30; Sun 5:30-10
Closed Thanksgiving, Christmas, New Year's Day   Wine and beer
Reservations accepted   Parking in the plaza
DC, MC, V   Low to moderate

The exciting cuisine found here is prepared by a woman chef who combines Jordanian recipes with French sauces. Don't miss the *bourak* (grilled beef wrapped in filo dough); grilled eggplant; stuffed vegetables with date sauce; chicken and rice "cake" surrounded by raspberry sauce; spicy shrimp; and Cornish hens. Some entrées are $8.95-9.95.

Kim's Restaurant   Vietnamese
745 First Street (Lumberyard Shopping Center)
Encinitas 92024   942-4816

M 11-9; Tu-Th 11-9:30; F 11-10; Sat 12-10; Sun 12-9
Closed major holidays   Wine and beer
Reservations accepted   Free parking in lot
MC, V   Low to low moderate

Kim's is the best Vietnamese restaurant in North County. Extensive menu includes very good spring rolls, stuffed grape leaves, stuffed crêpes, whole roasted Cornish hens, lemon grass chicken, and steamed fish. Fresh food, beautifully prepared.

La Bonne Bouffe   French provincial
471 Encinitas Blvd. (Town and Country Shopping Cntr.)
Encinitas 92024   436-3081

Tu-Sun 5:30-10
Closed major holidays   Wine and beer
Reservations accepted   Parking in front
All major credit cards   Moderate to expensive

This French provincial restaurant deserves its excellent reputation. Beef bourguignon, rack of lamb, frog legs and sweet breads (in season), duck in peppercorn sauce, Dover sole, and filet mignon are prepared in time-honored tradition. Intimate, European room. Consistently fine.

La Paloma
116 Escondido Avenue, Vista 92084

Gourmet Mexican
758-7140

M-Th 11-9; F 11-10; Sat 4-10; Sun 4-9
Closed July 4, Thanksgiving, Christmas
Reservations accepted
All major credit cards

Full bar
Free parking
Low to moderate

Applause goes to this gourmet Mexican restaurant for its presentation, unique recipes, and modest prices. The lobster-shrimp fajitas made *Gourmet* magazine. Shrimp and chicken cilantro and chiles rellenos are noteworthy, as are the Cuban-style black beans, albondigas soup, and turkey carnitas. Serves the best paella in North County. A treat.

Le Bambou
2634 Del Mar Heights Rd., Del Mar 92014

Nouvelle Vietnamese
259-8138

Tu-F 11:30-2, 5:30-9:30; Sat-Sun 5:30-9:30
Open all holidays
Reservations accepted
MC, V

Wine and beer
Free parking
Moderate

The nouvelle Vietnamese cuisine prepared here is fresh, light, and delicate. Portions are small—two people should order three entrées for a satisfactory meal. Soups are outstanding. The imperial rolls, lemon grass chicken, charbroiled pork, and catfish remain interesting.

Mandarin Garden
Mandarin Chinese, dim sum
Mira Mesa Mall, 8242 Mira Mesa Blvd. (Mira Mesa)
San Diego 92111

566-4720

M-F 11:30-2:30, 4:30-9; Sat-Sun 11:30-2:30, 4:30-10
Closed Thanksgiving, Christmas
Reservations accepted
All major credit cards

Full bar
Parking in mall lot
Low to low moderate

Exotic dishes and hard-to-find entrées and appetizers make this restaurant worth seeking out, especially at dinner. (Lunch offers standard Chinese food.) Extensive menu with many unusual appetizers. Attractive dim sum Saturday and Sunday. Try whole steamed fish, spicy twice-cooked pork, eel in brown sauce.

Mandarin Shogun
600 East Vista Way, Vista 92084

Japanese
758-8288

Tu-Th 11:30-2, 5-9:30; F 11:30-2, 5-10; Sat 5-10; Sun 5-9:30
Closed Thanksgiving, Christmas   Wine and beer
Reservations accepted   Parking in lot
MC, V   Low to expensive

Over 100 items are available, including sushi and cooked dishes. Make a meal from the extensive hot appetizer list or try the combination plate. Huge portions; pleasant food.

Ming Court
Cantonese/Mandarin Chinese
Country Plaza Center, 12750 Carmel Country Road
Del Mar 92130   793-2933

M-Th 11:30-10; F 11-11; Sat 12-11; Sun 2-10
Closed Thanksgiving   Full bar
Reservations accepted   Free parking
All major credit cards   Moderate to expensive

An elegant restaurant with stunning art objects, Ming Court serves wonderful Cantonese/Mandarin cuisine. Especially recommended: cilantro chicken, pungent shrimp, three-mushroom delight, and tangerine beef. Some tables have a view of the city. Piano bar Friday and Saturday nights. Festive.

Neiman's at the Twin Inns
American
2978 Carlsbad Boulevard, Carlsbad 92008   729-4131

Daily 5-9 (5-10 in summer); Sun brunch 9:30-2
Open all holidays   Full bar
Reservations for 10 or more; banquet   Parking in lot
   facilities available
AE, MC, V   Moderate to expensive

If you are nostalgic for the chicken dinners the Twin Inns used to serve, enjoy them in the main dining room for Sunday brunch, which also includes a large buffet. During the week, competent American cuisine is available. The high-peaked room with its turrets will enhance your meal. The Café, in the bar, offers a more limited menu.

Nobu Japanese Restaurant   Gourmet Japanese
315 South Highway 101, Solana Beach 92075   755-0113

Daily 11:30-2:30, 5-10
Open all holidays   Full bar
Reservations accepted (not for sushi bar)   Parking in mall lot
AE, MC, V   Low to moderate

The menu offers 40 sushi items, 18 stunning appetizers, and many entrées, including nine-course feasts and box dinners. Try rainbow salad, a baked crab dish named Dynamite, asparagus wrapped around beef, grilled yellowtail, and noodle dishes. All-you-can-eat lunch buffet M-F includes sushi.

Oscar's   American
1505 Encinitas Blvd., Encinitas 92024   632-0222

M-Th 10:30-9; F-Sat 10:30-10
Closed July 4, Christmas   No alcohol
No reservations   Parking in front/side
AE, MC, V   Low

It's fun for a casual meal and a few notches above fast food. The menu consists of pizza, barbecue, sandwiches, and salads. Best bet: chicken and rib combination served with enormous bowl of salad and hot bread. Thick slices of potatoes are à la carte.

Peter Chang's   Natural Chinese
1441 Encinitas Blvd., Encinitas 92024   942-5159

Daily 11:30-9:30
Closed Thanksgiving, Christmas   Full bar
Reservations accepted   Free parking
All major credit cards   Low to moderate

You must look carefully to find this place, but the natural Chinese cooking (no MSG or starch in the sauces on request) is a cut above most. The all-you-can-eat lunch buffet M-F ($4.50) provides 10 items plus California sushi roll, but it's tasty only if you arrive early. For dinner, try sautéed shrimp, string beans, chicken in plum sauce. Or ask Mr. Chang to cook for you. Buffet weekdays; regular lunch menu Saturday and Sunday.

Pizza Bozza
Pizza, pasta

429 Encinitas Blvd., Encinitas 92024   436-8664

M-Sat 11-10
Closed Easter, Thanksgiving, Christmas   Wine and beer
No reservations   Parking in lot
Discover, MC, V   Low to moderate

For unusual pizzas, antipasti, and pastas, try this dining room.
The pizzas are outstanding, especially the pizza *rustica* with
sliced fresh tomatoes and two cheeses (Abruzzi-style pizza has
no tomato sauce). Pastas include black wrinkled olives. The food
is unique. No foodie should miss this café.

Pisces Delicacies of the Sea
Gourmet fish/

La Costa Spa, 2100 Costa Del Mar Road   seafood
Carlsbad 92008   438-9111

M-Tu, Th-Sat 6:30 pm-9 pm   Jacket & tie for men
Closed Christmas   Full bar
Reservations required   Valet parking
All major credit cards   Expensive

In existence for two decades, this excellent restaurant is now
located at the spa itself. Fresh Maine lobster, lobster Thermidor,
Maryland soft-shell crabs, abalone, and Dover sole are its
hallmark dishes. Some items, such as the Caesar or wilted
spinach salads, are prepared only for two. A bit pricey and staid,
but you pay for tableside service and items flown in from distant
shores.

Potato Shack Café
American breakfast

120 West I St. (off First St.), Encinitas 92024   436-1282

M-F 7-2; Sat-Sun 7-3
Closed Thanksgiving, Christmas   No alcohol
No reservations   Street and lot parking
No credit cards   Low

A potato lover's heaven. You may have American fries, French
fries, baked potatoes, potato patties, potato salad, or potatoes
covered with various toppings. American fries are
all-you-can-eat. Omelets and hot cakes are huge. A great place
for children.

The Quail's Inn
1035 La Bonita Dr., San Marcos 92069

American
744-2445

M-Sat 11-9; Sun 9:30-9
Open all holidays
Reservations accepted for 6 or more
AE, MC, V

436-2445,
Full bar
Parking in front
Low to expensive

It's worth the ride to dine in this charming location on a picture-postcard lake. Invariably crowded and for good reason, the Inn offers fresh American fare: fish, seafood, prime rib, steaks. Dinner entrées include an all-you-can-eat salad bar. Arrive early for Sunday all-you-can-eat buffet that includes seafood for $10.95.

Real Texas BBQ
6904 Miramar Rd. (Miramar), SD 92121
Branch at 3755 Murphy Canyon Rd. 92123

Texas barbecue
566-5235
467-9074

M-F 10:30-9; Sat-Sun 11:30-9; branch closed Sun
Closed major holidays
Reservations for 6 or more
MC, V

Wine and beer
Free parking
Low

The Texas-style barbecue offers meat, chicken, links, and ribs. All-you-can-eat barbecue dinner ($10.95) includes side dishes plus beer, soft drink, tea, or coffee. It's served 6-9 pm M-F and all day Saturday and Sunday. Don't miss the succulent half-and-half sandwich (pork and beef brisket). Unadorned room but very clean. Same menu all day.

Red Tracton's
550 Via de la Valle, Del Mar 92014

Steaks, seafood
755-6600

M-Th 11-10; F-Sat 11-11; Sun 4-10
Closed Christmas
Reservations accepted
All major credit cards

Full bar
Valet and self parking
Moderate to expensive

Mammoth portions of prime rib, steak, chicken, and fish. Dinners come with corn on the cob, baked potatoes or vegetables; salads are à la carte. Each portion is enough for two. Lovely surroundings. Always crowded.

Samurai Japanese Restaurant   Gourmet Japanese
Lomas Santa Fe Plaza, 979 Lomas Santa Fe Drive
Solana Beach 92075   481-0032

M-F 11:30-2:30, 5-10 (F till 10:30); Sat 5-10:30; Sun 4-9:30
Closed Thanksgiving, Christmas   Full bar
Reservations accepted   Free parking
AE, MC, V   Moderate to expensive

Samurai boasts of "the largest sushi bar in California," plus a
menu of over 100 items. The food is artistically prepared, the
sushi uniformly fine, and there are three separate dining areas. A
meal of several appetizers is both interesting and satisfying.

Scalini   Northern Italian
3790 Via de la Valle, Del Mar 92014   259-9944

M 5:30-10; Tu-F 11:30-1:30, 5:30-10; Sat-Sun 5:30-10
Closed Thanksgiving, Christmas, New Year's Day   Full bar
Reservations accepted   Valet and self parking
All major credit cards   Upper moderate to expensive

Located on the road to Rancho Santa Fe, this handsome dining
room, a flight up, may offer a view of colorful, hot air balloons.
The best items here are the pasta dishes. Mesquite-grilled
preparations are as flavorful as those in sauces.

Spices Thai Café   Gourmet Thai
Piazza Carmel Shopping Center, 3810 Valley Centre Dr.
Del Mar 92014   259-0889

Daily 11-10
Closed July 4, Thanksgiving, Christmas   Wine and beer
Reservations accepted   Parking in mall lot
All major credit cards   Low to moderate

Thai cuisine at its best, containing no MSG and very little fat, is
served here. Seafood dishes rate high, especially seafood
panang, which contains shrimp, crab legs, scallops, and mussels.
Among other delicacies are duck, frog legs, and soft-shell crabs.
It's all superb. Put Spices Thai at the top of your list.

Star of India Restaurant
927 First Street, Encinitas 92028

Indian
632-1113

M 5-9:30; Tu-F 11:30-2:30, F-9:30 (F till 10): Sat-Sun 11:30-3, 5-10
Open all holidays
Reservations accepted
All major credit cards

Full bar
Free parking
Low to upper moderate

Authentic and well-flavored soups, rice, and vegetarian dishes, as well as tandoori chicken and lamb, are perennial favorites. All-you-can-eat buffet lunch, M-F ($6.95); Saturday and Sunday brunch with champagne or soft drink provides a wonderful alternative to ordinary fare ($9.50).

Stella's Hideaway Polish Restaurant
Peñasquitos Village Center, 14323 Peñasquitos Drive
Rancho Peñasquitos 92129

Polish

672-3604

Tu-Th 5-9:30; F 5-10; Sat 4-10; Sun 4-9
Closed major holidays
Reservations accepted for 6 or more
All major credit cards

Full bar
Parking in mall lot
Moderate

A mom-and-pop dining room, Stella's serves home-style sauerkraut, dill pickle soup, and 18 pungent entrées. Among the best are *rouladen* (beef roll-up), the Polish plate combination, and the boneless chicken breasts. Robust food, large portions. Entrées include soup or salad plus dessert. You'll enjoy yourself here.

Taryn's at the Track
514 Via de la Valle, Del Mar 92014

California
481-8300

Tu-Sun 5:30-9:30 (bar opens at 4:30)
Open major holidays
Reservations requested on weekends
AE, MC, V

Full bar
Parking in front
Low to low moderate

The best bet is the early bird special served Tuesday-Sunday 5:30-7 pm for $9.95. It offers salad plus a choice of entrées, such as King salmon, filet steak, baby back ribs, shrimp, pasta, or fresh fish, all with vegetables. Excellent value. Arrive early and be sure you're seated before 7 pm. Charming room; individual service.

Valentino's
Italian

Mercado Shopping Center, 11828 Rancho Bernardo Road
Rancho Bernardo 92128   451-3200

M-F 11-2, 5-9 (F till 10): Sat 5-10
Closed major holidays   Full bar
Reservations recommended   Free parking
Most major credit cards   Moderate to expensive

Valentino's has a lovely interior, good salads and pastas
(especially cannelloni) and a fine dish called Chicken Vesuvio.
The best bet is the lunch served M-F; it costs $5 and includes
salad and choice of nine pastas.

XpreZZO's Coffee House-Café
Coffeehouse

Ralph's Shopping Center, 15717 Bernardo Heights
   Parkway (at Pomerado Road)
Rancho Bernardo 92128   485-8055

M-Th 8 am-10 pm; F-Sat 8 am-12 midnight; Sun 9-3
Open all holidays   Wine and beer
Reservations accepted for 8 or more   Parking in mall lot
CB, DC, MC, V   Low

Champagne and wine, as well as a fireplace, upholstered chairs,
bookcases, French doors, and live music several nights a week,
make you forget that the location is a shopping center. Light
meals include egg dishes, quiche, salads. Dinner offers
specialties such as white bean and sausage cassoulet. Family
events on holidays. The ultimate coffeehouse-café.

Best Pizza
Del Mar Pizza, Del Mar 92
Pizza Bozza, Encinitas 100
Sammy's Woodfired Pizza, La Jolla 77
Sorrentino's, Clairemont 109
Tosca's Pasta and Pizza, Pacific Beach 62
The Venetian, Pt. Loma 62

Smart Dining
in
North City Mesas

Clairemont
Kearny Mesa
University City

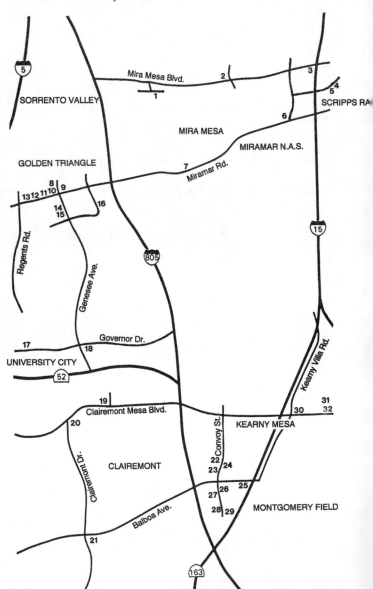

Open hours, menus, and prices change without notice. *Always call first.*

Map not exactly to scale.

Hsu's Szechuan Cuisine Hazard Village

Chinese, Szechuan, Mandarin, Hunan

9350 F-G Clairemont Mesa Boulevard (Kearny Mesa)
San Diego 92123   279-9799

M-F 11:15-9:30; Sat-Sun 11:15-10
Closed Thanksgiving   Full bar
Reservations accepted for 6 or more   Parking in lot
MC, V   Low to moderate

This restaurant features over 100 dishes, including Szechuan, Mandarin, and Hunan specialties.

Signature Dishes: Mongolian barbecue (beef, pork, or chicken); spicy chicken with orange; shrimp in Szechuan hot sauce; eggplant with ginger (with meat or vegetarian); fish filets with garlic sauce; whole steamed fish with garlic-wine sauce; fresh asparagus with shrimp (seasonal); seafood in a basket. **Dining Tip:** Call several hours in advance to order from the banquet menu: chicken in wine sauce; fresh abalone (when available); shark fin soup. Request no MSG.

Korea House

Korean

4620 Convoy Street (Kearny Mesa)
San Diego 92111   560-0080

M-F 10-10; Sat-Sun 12-10
Closed Thanksgiving   Full bar
Reservations accepted   Parking in lot
All major credit cards   Low to moderate

Remains one of the best Korean restaurants in the city. The setting is unusual: grotto, organist, chandeliers, and cooking vents to carry off fumes. You may dine at conventional tables, at barbecue tables, or on the floor.

Signature Dishes: Thin slices of beef or chicken to barbecue at your table; spicy seafood casserole with shrimp, crab, octopus, clams; *mandu* (Korean-style won tons in garlicky beef broth); spicy steamed mackerel; stir-fried octopus with vegetables. Entrées include 10 side dishes. Sushi bar. **Dining Tip:** Lots of garlic and chiles characterize this cuisine. If you wish to avoid these seasonings, barbecue at your table or ask for any fish on the menu grilled without spices.

Sorrentino's Ristorante Italiano Northern Italian

Diane Shopping Center, 4724 Clairemont Mesa
  Boulevard (Clairemont)
San Diego 92117   483-1811

Daily 4:30-9:30
Closed major holidays   Full bar
Reservations accepted   Parking in lot
Major credit cards (not Discover)   Moderate

Excellent family restaurant.

Signature Dishes: Appetizers: Focaccia bread with cheeses and
pine nuts; grilled red peppers with pesto and mozzarella cheese.
Entrées: Tortelloni with porcini mushrooms; chicken breast with
cheeses; shrimp with mushrooms and garlic; *pappardelle
Magdelena* (noodles with fresh, diced, uncooked tomatoes).
Dining Tip: This restaurant produces some of the best pizza in
the city: Pepperoni; four cheeses; spinach with fresh tomatoes;
or you name it, they'll play it. First-rate Italian sandwiches.
Take-out next door.

Szechuan Restaurant   Szechuan Chinese

4577 Clairemont Drive (Clairemont)
San Diego 92117   270-0251

M-Th 11:30-2:30, 5-10; F 11:30-2:30, 5-11; Sat 5-11; Sun 2-10
Closed Thanksgiving   Wine and beer
Reservations accepted   Free parking in lot
MC, V   Moderate

Dining rooms are available both upstairs and down—the one
upstairs is more attractive. The menu offers 120 items. Congenial
surroundings, intelligent waiters, good value.

Signature Dishes: Peking duck, Imperial whole fish, ginger
beef, string bean sauté with meat sauce, and General Tso's
chicken. The seafood in bird's nest (finely cut potatoes filled with
scallops, shrimp, and squid) is one of the best in the city.
Dining Tip: For a party of 6 or more arrange for a Chinese
banquet. Request no MSG.

Emerald Chinese Seafood Restaurant
Hong Kong fish/seafood

Pacific Gateway Plaza, 3709 Convoy St. (Kearny Mesa)
San Diego 92111   565-6888

M-F 11-3 (dim sum and lunch), 4-12 (F till 1 am); Sat 10-3, 4-1 am;
    Sun 10 am-12 midnight

Open all holidays	Wine and beer
Reservations accepted	Parking in front
All major credit cards	Upper moderate to expensive

Without a doubt the best Chinese restaurant for fresh seafood and fish. Superb Hong Kong chef. Fresh fish, prawns, and lobsters are kept in tanks and prepared when you order. Excellent lobster, scallops, honey-walnut shrimp, crab, and clams. Dim sum served daily; it's particularly fine on Sunday when 100 items are available plus your special requests.

The Good Egg
American Breakfast

7947 Balboa Ave. (Kearny Mesa), SD 92111   565-4244

Daily 6:30 am-2 pm

Closed Thanksgiving, Christmas	No alcohol
Reservations accepted for 8 or more	Parking in lot
Discover, MC, V	Low

The three-page menu offers eggs in a skillet; omelets; gourmet pancakes; waffles; several frittatas, including vegetarian; and freshly squeezed fruit juices. Long list of sandwiches for lunch.

Hideyoshi Japanese Restaurant
Japanese

Hazard Village, 9340-B Clairemont Mesa Boulevard
San Diego 92123 (Kearny Mesa)   569-9595

M-Sat 11-3, 3-10

Closed major holidays	Wine and beer
Reservations accepted	Parking in lot
DC, JCB, MC, V	Low to expensive

Fine sushi bar and unusual appetizers. For entrées, select sukiyaki, broiled salmon or yellowtail, chicken katzu, or Taiko Special feast for two or more. Visually and gastronomically a treat. Operated by two lovely women. High standards.

Kobe Misone
Japanese steak house

5451 Kearny Villa Road (Kearny Mesa)
San Diego 92123   560-7399

Tu-F 11:30-2, 5:30-10; Sat 5:30-10; Sun 5:30-9
Closed major holidays   Full bar
Reservations required   Parking in lot
AE, DC, JBC, MC, V   Low to expensive

Essentially a Japanese steak house. Entrées include soup, salad, and Japanese-style vegetables. You dine communally at the cooking tables. Food is well seasoned, especially with pepper.

Khyber Pass
Afghan

Empire Square, 4647 Convoy Street (Kearny Mesa)
San Diego 92111   571-3749

M-Sat 11;2:30, 5-10; Sun 5-10
Open all holidays   Wine and beer
Reservations accepted   Free parking
All major credit cards   Low to moderate

The Afghan food is consistently high in quality and taste appeal. Try the unusual appetizers, as well as the five-bean soup. Chicken with saffron rice, chicken curry, and lamb stew are recommended, as are beef with lentils and the four styles of rice: white, saffron, green (with spinach juice), and red (with cherry juice). Vegetarian plates available. All-you-can-eat lunch buffet.

Lorna's Italian Kitchen
Italian, pizza

Vons Shopping Center, 3945 Governor Drive
San Diego 92122 (University City)   452-0661

M-Th 11-9:30; F 11-10:30; Sat 4-10:30; Sun 4-9
Closed major holidays   Wine and beer
Reservations not accepted   Parking in lot
Discovery, MC, V   Low to moderate

Twenty pasta dishes are prepared here, all from scratch, as well as hot sandwiches, pizza, calzone. Good hearty food, specially the calzone stuffed with chicken and cheese, and the massive pizzas. Two seating areas. Crowded on weekends with students and families.

Mandarin Wok   Mandarin & Szechuan Chinese
4227 Balboa Ave. (Clairemont), SD 92117   272-3972

Tu-Th 11-9:30; F-Sat 11-10:30; Sun 12-9:30
Closed Thanksgiving; dinner only other holidays   Wine and beer
Reservations accepted   Free parking
MC, V   Low to moderate

The Chinese-born chef has spent years in Korea, Taiwan, and Japan and provides interesting accents to basic Mandarin and Szechuan cooking. Try the war wan ton soup (with egg whites); crispy beef in hot sauce; tung ting shrimp with barbecued pork; lemon chicken; and soft and hard noodles heaped with shrimp, beef, and chicken. Huge, attractive portions (two dishes will serve three); impeccable table settings. Take-out service.

Meiki Japanese Restaurant   Japanese
and Sushi Bar   566-0206
9823 Carroll Canyon Rd. (Scripps Ranch), SD 92131

Daily 11-4, 4-10
Closed July 4, Thanksgiving, Christmas, New Year's Day   Full bar
Reservations accepted   Free parking
All major credit cards   Low to moderate

A first-rate sushi bar with 42 items, Meiki is tucked away in a tiny shopping center. The fresh yellowtail, scallops in spicy sauce (*hotategai*), and baked salmon roll are wonderful. Cooked combination plates don't disappoint. Try this one.

The Original Pancake House   American breakfast
3906 Convoy St. (Kearny Mesa), SD 92111   565-1740

Daily 7-3
Closed Christmas   No alcohol
Reservations unnecessary   Free parking
DC, MC, V   Low

The unique apple pancake, an enormous puffy soufflé, should win a prize. Several varieties of pancakes are offered, including Swedish. Omelets cover an entire plate. Coffee arrives with whipping cream. Excellent spot for children as well as sensuous adults. Only limitation is early closing.

Papalulu
American Southwestern

3368 Governor Dr. (Univsity City), SD 92122   453-4844

Daily 7:30-11, 11-4:30, 4:30-9 (F-Sat till 10)
Closed July 4, Thanksgiving, Christmas   Wine and beer
Reservations accepted   Parking in mall lot
Discover, MC, V   Low

The eclectic menu includes Mexican influences, Southwestern flavors, Jamaican seasoning, and American vegetarian dishes. Best sellers are the spinach burger; Baja vegetarian lasagne made with *masa* (corn meal), fresh corn, cheese, noodles, and fresh tomato sauce; *papadilla* (flour tortillas stuffed with mashed potatoes and covered with cheeses and salsa). Massive portions.

Phuong Trang
Vietnamese

4170 Convoy St. (Kearny Mesa), SD 92111   565-6750

Sun-Th 9:30-11, 11-9:30; F-Sat 9-11, 11-10
Closed Chinese New Year   Wine and beer
Reservations accepted   Parking in lot
DC, MC, V   Low

One of the two best Vietnamese restaurants in the city, Phuong Trang offers 224 items. The healthy cuisine is pleasing to the eye as well as the palate. Best bets are egg rolls, char-grilled shrimp on sugar cane, ground beef wrapped in grape leaves, prawn salad, rice in earthenware pot, grilled whole fish, spring rolls. The breakfast (9-11) offers a variety of soups and rice dishes; unusual but stimulating. Swift service; highly palatable food.

Savoy Restaurant
Vietnamese, Chinese

4690 Convoy St. (Kearny Mesa), SD 92111   495-9139

Daily 11-4, 4-9:30 (F-Sat till 10:30)
Closed Thanksgiving   Wine and beer
Reservations accepted for 6 or more   Free parking
MC, V   Low

The setting is plain, but the Chinese and Vietnamese food could grace a more opulent stage. Delights include garlic shrimp, General Chao's chicken, snow pea plant (special vegetarian dish), Vietnamese spring roll, chicken, beef, and shrimp with soft noodles. Ask the owner, Lisa, for suggestions.

Thai House Cuisine
Gourmet Thai
4225 Convoy St. (Kearny Mesa), SD 92111   278-1800

M-Th 11-3, 5-10; F-Sat 11-3, 5-11; Sun 4-10
Closed major holidays   Wine and beer
Reservations accepted   Parking in lot
DC, MC, V   Low moderate to expensive

Not to be confused with Thai House in Point Loma, this attractive Thai restaurant serves fine gourmet specialties. Avoid dishes where tofu takes the place of seafood or duck. Do try other vegetarian offerings, the Thai Boat filled with seafood, chicken with basil, whole fish preparations, and ground shrimp and chicken. Extensive menu; superior service.

General Dining Tip: When dining in any Asian restaurant, always inquire about MSG and request that it not be used. Many people are allergic to it.

Best Breakfasts
Harry's Café Gallery, La Jolla 72 • **Kono's**, Pacific Beach 59
Santa Clara Grill, Mission Beach 55
Potato Shack Café, Encinitas 100 • **Hob Nob Hill**, Banker's Hill 42
The Good Egg, Kearny Mesa 110
The Original Pancake House, Kearny Mesa 112

Best Coffeehouses
Baked by Etta. La Jolla 70 • **Extraordinary Desserts**, San Diego 41
Gelato Vero Caffe, Mission Hills 42 • **La Tazza**, Downtown 25
The Pannikin Café, La Jolla 75
Pannikin's Brockton Villa, La Jolla 75 • **Quel Fromage**, Hillcrest 44
Sarah Bernhardt's, Normal Heights 127 • **The Study**, Hillcrest 46
Village Emporium, La Mesa 128
XpreZZO's Coffee House-Café, Rancho Bernardo 104

High Tea
U. S. Grant Hotel, 326 Broadway, 232-3121, Tu-Sat 3-6
Westgate Hotel, 1055 Second Avenue, 238-1818, M-Sat 2:30-5
Horton Grand Hotel, 311 Island Avenue (at Third),
544-1886, Tu-Sat 2:30-5

Smart Dining
in
East Suburbs

Alpine
East San Diego
La Mesa
Lemon Grove
Normal Heights
Santee
State College

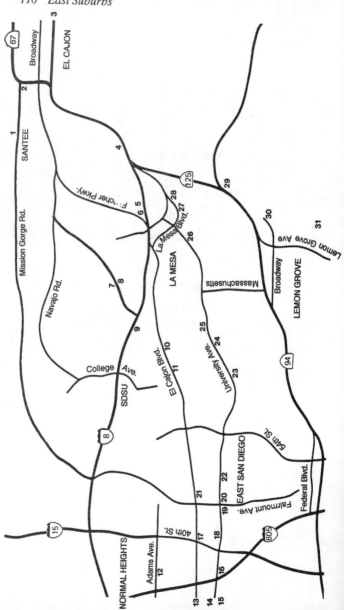

Open hours, menus, and prices change without notice. *Always call first.*

Map not exactly to scale.

Camelot   Vietnamese
6942 University Avenue
La Mesa 91941   462-0042

Tu-Th 11-9; F-Sat 11-10; Sun 11-9
Open all holidays   Wine and beer
Reservations accepted   Parking in lot
Discover, MC, V   Low

One of the two best Vietnamese restaurants in the San Diego area.
The 215 menu items include 35 soups and as many rice dishes.
First-rate dining. Service includes hot towels and change of
plates for each course.

Signature Dishes: Spring rolls; grape leaves stuffed with beef;
ground shrimp on sugar cane; Vietnamese omelet; chicken soup
with fish, shrimp, and noodles (a meal in itself); lemon grass
chicken; whole steamed fish with ginger; rice in earthenware pot.

Dining Tip: The owner will gladly make suggestions if you are
a first-time diner. He will remember your favorites on subsequent
visits.

Dansk Restaurant   Scandinavian
8425 La Mesa Boulevard
La Mesa 91941   463-0640

Tu-Th 8-3; F-Sat 8-3, 5-9; Sun 8-3
Closed Christmas   Wine and beer
Reservations accepted for dinner only   Parking in lot
All major credit cards   Low to moderate

The breakfast and lunch menus include first-rate waffles,
Swedish pancakes, omelets, and open-faced sandwiches. Dinner
offers Scandinavian specialties. Devoted service; highly
satisfying food. Outdoor and indoor dining.

Signature Dishes (F and Sat dinner only): Midnight sun
Norwegian salmon with three sauces (shallot, red, and yellow
bell peppers); Swedish-style lamb with coffee cognac sauce
flamed at the table; tenderloin of pork stuffed with prunes and
apples plus red cabbage; shrimp in Aquavit with three styles of
rice; Swedish meatballs; Swedish-style stuffed cabbage in dill
sauce. All dinners include soup or salad. **Dining Tip:** If you're
on a budget, stay with the highly satisfying dinners for $9.95.

Lader's Italian-Californian Restaurant

5654 Lake Murray Boulevard   Northern Italian
La Mesa 91941   463-9919

Tu-F 11:30-3, 3--9:30; Sat-Sun 4-10
Closed Thanksgiving, Christmas   Wine and beer
Reservations accepted   Parking in mall lot
MC, V   Low

A charming dining room, Lader's offers hearty recipes from
southern Italy and elegant ones from the north. Entrées include
soup or salad. Pizza available for take-out only.

Signature Dishes: Seafood Provençal (shrimp, New Zealand
mussels, clams); chicken Florentine with spinach, sun dried
tomatoes and mozzarella; stuffed eggplant with two cheeses;
fettucine with basil, pine nuts, and tomatoes; sautéed chicken
with artichokes; Maryland crab cakes; grilled escalar fish; jumbo
scallops. **Dining Tip:** Come here on Sunday for a relaxed family
meal.

A Dong   Vietnamese

3874 Fairmount Avenue (East San Diego)
San Diego 92105   298-4420

Daily 9 am-10 pm
Open all holidays   Wine and beer
Reservations accepted for large parties   Free parking in lot
All major credit cards   Low

The menu runs to 200 items! You won't be disappointed in the
spring rolls; ground shrimp on sugar cane; charbroiled, stuffed
grape leaves; chicken lemon grass with red chiles; fried rice in
earthenware pot; or the ancient hot pot. Items may not arrive in
the sequence in which they were ordered.

Alpine Inn
American beef

2225 Alpine Boulevard, Alpine 91901   445-5172

M-F 11-11; Sat-Sun 9-11
Open all holidays   Full bar
Reservations not accepted   Parking in rear lot
All major credit cards   Low moderate to expensive

If you're a beef lover, arrive on Sunday after 2:30 pm for the
mountaineer cut of prime rib. That day only you'll get huge
amounts of good beef plus baked potato for $10.95. Soup or salad
is included. Another good buy is the vast, tasty Texas burger
served on a Kaiser roll with steak fries. Low cost early bird dinner
offers salad plus choice of steak, ribs, or shrimp for $7.95.

Anthony's La Mesa
Fish/seafood

9530 Murray Drive, La Mesa 91942   463-0368

Daily 11:30-8:30
Closed Easter, most major holidays   Full bar
Reservations not accepted   Free parking in lot
All major credit cards   Moderate

Located on a spring-fed natural lake, Anthony's has an outdoor
patio where cocktails, appetizers, and lunch are available.
Regular Anthony's menu plus fresh fish market.

Arigato
Japanese

5575 Baltimore Dr., #110, La Mesa 91942   469-3157

M-F 11:30-3, 5-9; Sat 12-3, 5-9
Closed Thanksgiving, Christmas   Semi-full bar
Reservations not accepted   Parking in lot
No credit cards   Low

Here's a great bargain Japanese restaurant. The top price is $7.75
for the house special: New York steak, scallops, and vegetables.
Best bets include the combination plates which contain sesame
chicken, tempura, and gyoza dumplings. Food is fresh and
flavorful.

Asmara Restaurant
Ethiopian
4433 El Cajon Blvd. (East San Diego), SD 9210563-3666

Tu-Sun 12-10:30
Closed Christmas
Reservations unnecessary
No credit cards

Wine and beer
Street parking
Low

Try this immaculate Abyssinian/Ethiopian café. The menu is limited to beef, lamb, chicken, and vegetables; and the food is very spicy. No utensils are served; you pick up the food with *injera*, a spongy bread. College students frequent this place and like it because it's different. Try the *sambussa* (turnovers), chicken with hardboiled egg, lamb cubes, and vegetable platter.

Bessie's Garite
Southern
954 Cardiff St. (edge of Lemon Grove & Spring Valley)
Lemon Grove 92114
463-5539

Tu-F 11-2, 5-9; Sat 11-9; Sun 12-8
Closed Thanksgiving, Christmas
Reservations accepted
MC, V

Wine and beer
Free parking in lot
Low to low moderate

The best Southern food in San Diego is served here. The pork chops smothered with corn bread dressing and gravy are mouth watering; so is the fried chicken. Also delicious are hush puppies, ribs (on weekends), chitlins, catfish Creole dishes, and peach cobbler. Fried green tomatoes are available May through August. Wonderful, authentic food. Worth the effort to get here.

Canton Seafood Restaurant
Cantonese Chinese
4134 University Ave. (East SD), SD 92105   281-6008

Daily 11 am- 12 midnight
Call about holidays
Reservations not accepted
MC, V

Wine and beer
Free parking small lot
Low to moderate

The *dim sum* served M-F 11 am-3 pm is outstanding, but the variety increases on weekends. Arrive early on Sat or Sun for *dim sum* from 9 am-3 pm. At dinner, try whole fish in ginger, fresh clams, and scallops.

Chang Cuisine of China
Mandarin Chinese
5500 Grossmont Center Dr. (Grossmont Shopping Cntr.)
La Mesa 91942   464-2288

Sun-Th 11:30-9:30; F-Sat 12-10:30
Closed Thanksgiving   Full bar
Reservations accepted   Free parking in mall lot
All major credit cards   Low to moderate

The setting is very beautiful with lots of Chinese art, and the dishes are subtle rather than fiery. Try rainbow shrimp, twin delights (pork and chicken), and crispy beef. The string beans are excellent.

College Restaurant
American
6695 El Cajon Blvd. (State College), SD 92115 469-1140

Daily 6 am-8:30 pm
Closed Christmas   No alcohol
Reservations not accepted   Free parking in lot
MC, V   Low

A haven for those on a budget, this restaurant is noted for its fried chicken dinner, with choice of soup or salad, potatoes, and hot rolls. Not fancy, but plentiful and fresh. Chicken-fried steak is another staple. Home-style breakfasts.

D. Z. Akin
Jewish
Alvarado Plaza, 6930 Alvarado Road (State College)
San Diego 92120   265-0218

Sun-Th 7 am-9 pm (call for longer summer hours); F-Sat 7 am-11 pm
Closed Yom Kippur, Thanksgiving, Christmas   Wine and beer
Reservations accepted for 6 or more   Parking in front
MC, V   Low to moderate

Surely the best Jewish delicatessen in San Diego. Soups are wonderful and you have 110 sandwiches to choose from, all hefty enough to feed two. The chopped liver and knishes rival what Mother used to make; and kasha, kasha varnishkes, and potato pancakes are available daily. At dinner, try roast or fried chicken, roast brisket of beef, roast beef, liver and onions, meat loaf, or stuffed cabbage. Excellent bakery.

Fairouz Café and Gallery · Lebanese and Greek
8731 Broadway (at Spring), La Mesa 91941 · 697-2640

M-Sat 10-5, 5-9; Sun 10-8
Closed major holidays · No alcohol
Reservations not accepted · Street parking
No credit cards · Low to low moderate

A sister restaurant to the one on Midway, this 25-seats restaurant offers buffets for lunch and dinner and Greek and Lebanese items from the menu. Excellent food and service, but a mini-version of the original.

Hometown Buffet · American
University Square, 5881 University Ave. (State College)
San Diego 92120 · 583-7373

M-Sat 11-9; Sun 8 am-8:30 pm
Closed Christmas · No alcohol
Reservations not accepted · Parking in mall lot
All major credit cards · Low

If you long for cooking as it existed 50 years ago, try this all-you-can-eat low-cost ($6.95) buffet. Massive amounts of food that's fresh but not low-cal/low-cholesterol. Not for gourmet diners. Fun.

House of Canton · Chinese
8015 Broadway, Lemon Grove 91945 · 469-4757

Tu-Th 11:30-9:30; F 11:30-10:30; Sat 2-10:30; Sun 2-9:30
Open all holidays · Full bar
Reservations accepted for the Banquet Room · Free parking in lot
MC, V · Low to moderate

Seek out this Cantonese-Hunan restaurant for its Hunan scallops, Yu-Hsiang eggplant with pork, chef's fish in batter, pan-fried noodles, Mongolian pork chops, Peking duck, and whole, steamed fish. Very fine chef.

J-K's Greek Café
Greek

7749 University Avenue, La Mesa 91941   464-1915

M-F 11-8:30; Sat 11-9
Closed Christmas   Wine and beer (including Greek wine and beer)
Reservations accepted F and Sat   Parking in lot
No personal checks   Low

Try this family-owned café for tasty, fresh, home-style Greek cooking. Combination plates are inexpensive enough to double as appetizers if divided between two or more. Desserts prepared on the premises. Take-outs available.

Jyoti Bihanga
Vegetarian

3351 Adams Ave. (Normal Hghts.), SD 92116   282-4116

M-Tu 11-9; W 11-3; Th-F 11-9; Sat 7:30 am-8 pm; Sun 8-1 am
Closed Christmas, New Year's Day   No alcohol
Reservations not accepted   Street and lot parking
No credit cards   Low

Low-cost, tasty, and fresh vegetarian dishes with international influences. The mildly Indian ones include a different curry every other day. Soups, salads, and nightly specials are good bets. All-you-can-eat Sat morning buffet. Phone about hours as the café is open three Sundays during month.

Kooter's Bar-B-Que
Barbecue

70 Towne Center Parkway (left off Mission Gorge Road)
Santee 92071   562-7302

Sun-Th 11-10; F-Sat 11-11
Closed Thanksgiving, Christmas   Wine and beer
Reservations unnecessary   Free parking in lot
ATM, MC, V   Low

You'll love the immaculate, cheerful premises and the friendly service; but best of all is the barbecue. You won't go wrong with the barbecued beef sandwich, onion ring loaf, giant baked potato, and baby back ribs or chicken. Same menu lunch and dinner.

Little Italy
Italian

4367 University Ave. (at Fairmount in East San Diego)
San Diego 92105
281-4949

Daily 11 am-2 am
Closed Thanksgiving, Christmas
Reservations not accepted
AE, MC, V

Wine and beer
Parking in back
Low

This long-established restaurant offers spirited calzone and pizzas (with lots of stuffing and toppings), plus a bargain dinner for two ($10.50) including salad, cheese pizza, lasagne, spaghetti, garlic bread. Simple surroundings, hearty portions.

Ly's Garden
Chinese and Cambodian

6011 El Cajon Blvd. (State College), SD 92120 265-1885

Daily 12 noon-12 midnight
Open all holidays
Reservations accepted
All major credit cards

Full bar
Free parking in lot
Low to moderate

Chinese specials are available, but it's best to order the Cambodian food. Sure fire hits: fire pot soup (a variety of ingredients cooked in little baskets plunged into broth); salted shrimp; clams with ginger sauce; hot and sour shrimp; chicken with lemon grass; and beef with sour vegetables.

Mama's Bakery and Lebanese Delicatessen
4237 Alabama Street (south of El Cajon Blvd. in Normal
    Heights)
Lebanese
San Diego 92104
688-0717

Tu-Sat 10-6 (summer 10-7); Sun 8-2
Closed Christmas, New Year's Day
Reservations not accepted
No credit cards

No alcohol
Street parking
Low

For an unusual light meal or take-out, try the Lebanese sandwiches. Handmade whole wheat dough is rolled to the size of a small pizza, then filled with your choice of cheese, herbs, chicken, or beef and cooked on top of a special *sajj* oven. Wonderful texture and flavor. Patio dining only.

Mario's De La Mesa
Mexican

8187 Center Street, La Mesa 91942 · 461-9390

M 9:30-4; Tu-Sat 9:30-9:30; Sun 8:30-2:30
Open all holidays · Wine and beer
Reservations not accepted · Free street parking
No credit cards · Low

The food and value more than make up for the simple dining room located in an industrial area. You'll find the best tamales outside of Mexico and amazing shrimp with incomparable green salsa. The soups (which include menudo) are outstanding, as are the mole preparations. Sunday breakfast offers such hearty portions that you won't have to eat until dinner. Call for directions. A treasure of a café.

Nicolosi's
Italian

5351 Adobe Falls Rd. (Waring exit off I-8/State College)
San Diego 92120 · 287-5757

M-Th 11-9; F-Sat 11-10; Sun 12-9
Closed Easter, Christmas · Full bar
Reservations accepted Sun-Th for 8 or more · Parking in lot
AE, MC, V · Low

Nicolosi's has been serving good pizzas and terrific torpedo sandwiches for decades. Bargain favorites include a "pail of pasta" that serves at least four.

Red Sea Restaurant
Ethiopian

4717 University Ave. (East SD), SD 92105 · 285-9722

Daily 11-11
Call about holidays · Wine and beer
Reservations accepted · Parking in back
MC, V · Low

Students flock to this immaculate Ethiopian restaurant. All preparations are served over *injera*, a sponge-like bread that sops up gravies. Chicken *wat* (stew) with hard-boiled egg, *sambusa* (stuffed pastries) and the vegetarian plates are among your best bets.

Sarah Bernhardt's
Coffeehouse

3982 30th St. (Normal Heights), SD 92104   574-1585

Tu-F 8-5; Sat 8-6
Closed July 4, Thanksgiving, Christmas
Reservations not accepted
No credit cards

No alcohol
Street parking
Low

A cozy tea and coffee room, Sarah Bernhardt's serves superior desserts to eat there or take out. Cakes, pastries, and chocolate cakes are delectable. One of the few places that prepares authentic Danish pastry.

Sala Thai
Thai

Campus Plaza, 6161 El Cajon Boulevard (State College)
San Diego 92115   229-9050

M-Sat 11-10; Sun 5-10
Open all holidays
Reservations accepted
All major credit cards

Wine and beer
Free parking in lot
Low to low moderate

You will find this Thai restaurant as charming as its owner. The menu is extensive, the service attentive. Call a few hours in advance for Cornish hens, Seafood Delight in clay pot, fish cakes, or fish soufflé in banana leaves, as well as Thai standards and Chinese dishes. Extensive menu. Excellent service.

Valley House Restaurant
American

10767 Woodside Ave. (Mission Gorge Rd. becomes
   Woodside after Magnolia), Santee 92071   562-7878

Sun-Th 6:30 am-9 pm; F-Sat 6:30 am-10 pm
Open all holidays
Reservations accepted
MC, V

Full bar
Parking in lot
Low

You'll find your dream Iowa Porker here—pork tenderloin that's pounded, deep fried in batter, and served on a bun. It's juicy and succulent. W and F nights, all-you-can-eat fish and chips are $7.45. If you like biscuits and white gravy, this place is for you.

Vesuvio Italian Restaurant and Pizza House

3412 30th Street (Normal Heights)   Italian
San Diego 92104   291-3230

Sun-Th 11 am-1 am; F-Sat 11 am-3 am
Closed Easter, Thanksgiving, Christmas   Wine and beer
Reservations accepted for 4 or more   Street parking
No credit cards   Low to moderate

The daily lunch specials, served with salad and bread, start at
$3.95, and dinners in the dining room start at $6. The major asset
is the separate take-out service, which offers menu items plus
pizza to 1 am weekdays, 3 am on weekends.

Vicente's   Mexican barbecue

6315 University Avenue (State College)
San Diego 92115   287-4443

M-Sat 11-9
Closed Christmas   Wine and beer
Reservations accepted   Free parking in lot
No credit cards   Low to low moderate

Discover this small, immaculate, family-run restaurant that
serves excellent barbecue dishes and Mexican specialties at
amazingly low costs. The barbecue sampler with chicken, pork
ribs, beef short ribs, plus beans, rice, salsa, and tortillas easily
serves two. The carne asada is also recommended.

Village Emporium   Coffeehouse

8384 La Mesa Boulevard, La Mesa 91941   464-0611

Sun-Th 7 am-11 pm; F-Sat 7 am-12 midnight
Closed Thanksgiving, Christmas   No alcohol
Reservations accepted for 6 or more   Street parking
MC, V   Low

You'll enjoy this beautiful shop that offers retail items as well as
coffee, tea, and espresso. Menu includes turkey breast and roast
beef sandwiches, real Philly sandwich (beef, onions, cheese),
chef salad, fresh raw vegetable salad, chicken salad, daily soups,
bratwurst, and sauerkraut. Live music every night at 8 pm.

Smart Dining
in
Southbay and Coronado

Chula Vista
Coronado
National City

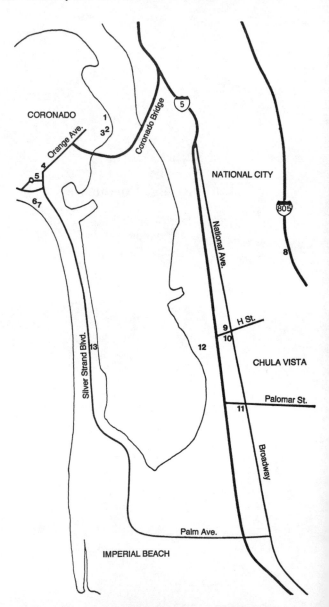

Open hours, menus, and prices change without notice. *Always call first.*

Map not exactly to scale.

Azzura Point Loew's   Pacific Rim
Coronado Bay Resort, 4000 Coronado Bay Road
Coronado 92118   424-4000

Sun-Th 6 pm-10 pm; F-Sat 6 pm-11 pm
Open all holidays   Full bar
Reservations strongly recommended   Validated parking
All major credit cards   Expensive

A romantic restaurant with a stunning bay view. The gourmet menu consists of Pacific Rim specialties: fish, seafood, meat, and pasta, many with Asian flavors. Rice and stir-fried vegetables are à la carte.

Signature Dishes: Hong Kong-style striped bass in cilantro sauce; Alaskan halibut with fennel and leeks; grilled yellowfin tuna; Canadian salmon; grilled loin of lamb; Black Angus New York strip; guinea hen. **Dining Tip:** Menus vary seasonally but steak, lamb, and fish remain constant. First courses are innovative—you can make a meal from corn soup with crab cake fritters, mixed field greens and lobster, or goat cheese chile relleno.

L'Escale   French
Le Meridian Hotel, 2000 Second Street
Coronado 92118   435-3000

M-F 6:30 am-10 pm; Sat-Sun 10:30-2:30
Open all holidays   Full bar
Reservations accepted;   Valet and validated parking
   recommended for Sun brunch
All major credit cards   Low moderate to expensive

A casual dining room in a first-rate hotel, L'Escale faces the pool. Take advantage of various fixed price meals, the jazz brunch served Sat or prize-winning all-you-can-eat Sun brunch.

Signature Dishes: Dinner: French onion soup; duck breast on couscous; lobster over linguine; grilled chicken with lemon grass sauce, grilled swordfish. **Dining Tip:** Sun night is "Family Night." Dinner for two is $30; every additional person $10. Meal includes soup or salad, entrée, dessert, and wine.

Marius
French provincial

Le Meridian Hotel, 2000 Second Street
Coronado 92118 435-3000

Tu-Sat 6-10
Open all holidays   Full bar
Reservations accepted weekends only   Valet and hotel lot parking
All major credit cards   Expensive

Open for dinner only, this gourmet room offers French provincial meals served in elegant surroundings.

Signature Dishes: The $49 fixed price meal may include spinach soup; green asparagus in puff pastry; Dover sole or Viennoisse pheasant; raspberry mousse; ginger crème brulée (add $20 for four "tastes" of appropriate wine—not full glasses). Every Thursday, the Tour de France meal offers three, four, or five courses for $39 to $59. **Dining Tip:** The fixed price meals may prove too expensive or provide too much food. An alternative is the Best of the Best menu, with favorites such as shellfish soup, sea scallops, lamb medallions.

Primavera Ristorante
Northern Italian

932 Orange Avenue
Coronado 92118 435-0454

M-F 11-2:30, 5-10; Sat-Sun 5-10
Closed major holidays   Full bar
Reservations accepted   Street parking and in rear
All major credit cards   Moderate to expensive

One of Coronado's best restaurants, this northern Italian venue features excellent pasta, seafood, fish, *risotto* (rice dishes), and various meats. Handsome setting, first-rate service, and a talented chef.

Signature Dishes: Pasta: Gnocchetti (potato dumplings) in shrimp sauce; tortellini with mushrooms; angel hair pasta with prosciutto and herbs. Entrées: Salmon Piedmontese (with shrimp and lobster sauce); *calamari* (squid) and clams with spinach; grilled lamb chops; swordfish with lemon capers; scallops in brandy. **Dining Tip:** Most items are relatively expensive, but the pasta dishes aren't too costly.

Barrio Fiesta of Manila
Gourmet Filipino
Town & Country Center, 1510-D Sweetwater Road
National City 91950   474-0177

M-Th 11-9:30; F-Sun 11-10   No alcohol
Closed Holy Thursday, Good Friday   Parking in lot
Reservations for 8 or more; 15% gratuity   AE, MC, V
     added to bill   Low to moderate

This mother of all Filipino restaurants serves gourmet food in a
beautiful room that resembles a garden. If you like the exotic, try
squid in garlic sauce, crispy *pata* (deep-fried pig's knuckle) and
kare-kare (meat stew with peanut sauce). More conservatively,
order crispy chicken, beef Tagalog, and possibly milkfish. Don't
overlook the noodle and rice dishes and lumpia egg rolls.

Casa Salsa
Mexican
625 H Street, Chula Vista 91910   420-3665

Daily 11 am-2 am
Open all holidays   Full bar
Reservations accepted   Free parking
AE, MC, V   Low to moderate

The bargain of this well-established, colorful Mexican restaurant
is the "taco fiesta", served on a lazy Susan that holds crocks of
shredded beef, seasoned chicken, carnitas, refried beans, cheese,
and hot tortillas. Three can eat heartily at minimal cost from this
make-your-own taco dish. The carne asada tacos and tostada
suprema are also worthwhile. Huge portions, swift service.

Center Cut Restaurant
American
534 Broadway, Chula Vista 91910   476-1144

M-Sat 11-9; Sun 10-9
Open all holidays   Full bar
Reservations accepted   Free parking
All major credit cards   Moderate to expensive

Straightforward, well-prepared American cuisine. Entrée prices
include soup or salad—select the salad. Specializes in steaks and
prime rib; the fish and seafood are also fine. Buy one dinner,
second one is $2.99. All-you-can-eat Sunday brunch for $6.95.

Chez Loma
Continental

1132 Loma Avenue, Coronado 92118
435-0661

M-F 5:30-10; Sat-Sun 10-2, 5:30-10
Closed Thanksgiving, Christmas
Reservations accepted
AE, DC, MC, V

Wine and beer
Street parking
Moderate to expensive

Located in a historical house, Chez Loma is noted for its duck in green/peppercorn sauce, fresh fish, and chicken dishes. Sat and Sun brunch, $9.95: juice or champagne and choice of 10 entrées, such as eggs Benedict or steak and eggs.

Crown Room
Continental

Hotel del Coronado, 1500 Orange Avenue
Coronado 92118
435-6611, ext. 7240

M-Sat 7-11, 11:30-3, 5-9:30; Sun 9-2, 5-10
Open all holidays
Reservations accepted
All major credit cards

Full bar
Self and valet parking
Moderate to expensive

A sunset dinner, consisting of straightforward cooking, is served M-Sat from 5-6:30 pm for $17.50. It costs $25 the rest of the evening and includes soup or salad, choice of two entrées, dessert, and coffee. The regular menu offers Continental specialties. Make early reservations for the Crown Room's lavish all-you-can-eat Sun brunch. Jacket and tie suggested.

Jake's South Bay
Fish/seafood

570 Marina Parkway, Chula Vista 91910
476-0400

M-F 11:15-2:30, 5-9:30 (F till 10); Sat 5-10; Sun 10-2:30, 4:30-9:30;
    Seafood Bar: 11:30-10 daily
Closed Thanksgiving, Christmas
Reservations accepted
AE, MC, V

Full bar
Free parking
Moderate to expensive

You can't ask for a more romantic setting in Chula Vista than this restaurant on Coronado Bay. The vistas are stunning and the boats anchored outside add local color. The menu is mostly fish and seafood, competent but not exciting in preparation. Sunday buffet brunch.

Koto
Japanese

651 Palomar Street, Chula Vista 91910

691-1418

Th-Tu 11:30-2, 5-10
Closed major holidays
Reservations for 8 or more
MC, V

Wine and beer
Free parking
Low to moderate

The outstanding features here are the *kama-meshi* rice dinners and about 20 unique appetizers. The combination entrées tend to be expensive and not as exciting. Beautiful sushi bar with excellent selections. Koto music played weekends. Very good food and uplifting experience.

Peohe's the Landing
Fish/seafood

1201 First Street, Coronado 92118

437-4474

M-F 11:30-2:30, 5:30-10 (F till 11); Sat 11:30-2:30, 5-11;
      Sun 10:30-10
Open all holidays
Reservations recommended
All major credit cards

Full bar
Call about parking
Moderate to expensive

This waterfront restaurant offers a gorgeous view, interior waterfalls, and fresh fish daily, some flown in from Hawaii. Try char-grilled escolar in Chinese pesto; char-grilled salmon in ginger-pepper; halibut *mai'a* (with bananas and macadamia nuts). Soup or salad à la carte. Sunday brunch features omelets, banana pancakes, eggs Benedict, and fish from the menu.

Prince of Wales Room
Continental

Hotel del Coronado, 1500 Orange Avenue
Coronado 92118

435-6611

Tu-Sun 6 pm-10 pm
Open all holidays
Reservations recommended
All major credit cards

Full bar
Self and valet parking
Expensive

The gourmet dining room of this venerable hotel boasts an old-fashioned windowless atmosphere and offers fine steaks, fresh fish and seafood, duck, and chicken. A new menu will be available in September with traditional as well as contemporary dishes. Jacket required, tie optional.

Smart Dining
in
Tijuana

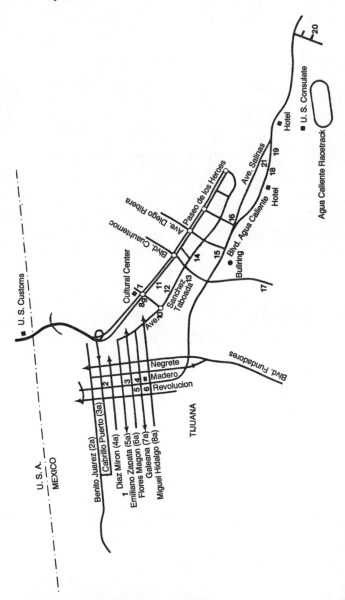

To reach Revolución from the border follow the signs marked "Centro" ("Downtown") to 3rd Street. Turn onto Revolución. At its south end Revolución bends east and becomes Agua Caliente.

To reach Zona Rio and the Cultural Center from the border, follow signs that say Zona Rio, Paseo de los Héroes.

To reach Avenida Sanchez Taboada take Paseo de los Héroes to the Cultural Center. Continue on Paseo de los Héroes until you pass the statue of the Indian, the statue of Abraham Lincoln, and you see the Hotel Lucerne. Go three blocks south of the Hotel Lucerne and make a left. You will then see the sign for Avenida Sanchez Taboada.

It's best to pay with American dollars, rather than convert to pesos. Most credit cards are accepted in the larger restaurants.

To telephone Tijuana use the international code: 011 + 52 + 66 + 6-digit number. When calling in Tijuana, use only the restaurant's 6-digit number.

Open hours, menus, and prices change without notice. *Always call first.*

Map not exactly to scale.

Birrieria Guanajuato
Baby goat only

Avenida Abraham Gonzalez 102, Colonia Francisco Villa
Tijuana   37-70-70

Daily 8-8   Low

Located high in the Tijuana hills, this café has a menu with two
items only. It's authentic, tasty, fresh, and unbelievably low in
cost. No-frills picnic tables and benches. Few Americans.

Signature Dishes: *Cabrito* (roasted baby goat) and *gorditas*
(melted cheese pancakes). **Dining Tip:** Be sure to arrive early,
before the food runs out. It's worth the effort.

Take downtown off ramp to Third. Consider Avenida Revolución
"A" Street. Count down the streets until you arrive at "H." Turn
left at "H," turn right on Fourth, go up the hill to Colonia
Altamira, then turn onto Francisco Villa. If you prefer, hire a taxi.

Buenos Aires
Argentinian

Paseo de los Héros 9415 (upstairs, Suite 8), Plaza Fiesta
Zona Rio, Tijuana   84-75-02

M-Sat 1-11   Low to low moderate

This charming Argentinian restaurant is located next door to La
Taberna Española but one flight up. You can opt either for safe,
slightly familiar dishes, or for the adventurous. The menu,
identical from opening to closing, is printed in Spanish. A waiter
will translate for you.

Signature Dishes: Soup, *empanadas*, cannelloni, and rolled
breast of chicken. For the exotic, order *plato Argentino*, a cold
appetizer plate with kidneys, pig's knuckles, tongue, and
assorted slices of meat stuffed with vegetables. Or try the
parrillada, grilled meats that include sweetbreads and steak.

Take Paseo de los Héroes to the Cultural Center. The Plaza Fiesta
is across the street on the right hand side.

Café La Especial
Mexican

718 Avenida Revolución (between Calle 3 and Calle 4)
Tijuana   85-66-54

Daily 9 am-10 pm   Low

It's halfway down a stairway on the east side of Revolución just below Third Street. A colorful shopping area exists below.

Signature Dishes: Hearty tacos, enchiladas, chiles rellenos, tamales, egg dishes, and steak have been prepared at this family café for decades.

Chiki-Jai
Spanish Basque

1050 Avenida Revolución (corner of Seventh)
Tijuana   85-49-55

Th-Tu 11-9   Low to moderate

Chiki-Jai is noted for its Basque-style food (Spanish, as distinct from Mexican). The setting is simple. During its many years, this restaurant has not capitulated to Americanization.

Signature Dishes: Squid in its own ink, Basque-style chicken, broiled mushrooms, and its trademark—hot crusty rolls served with blue cheese. Shrimp and filet mignon are also good choices.

El Faro De Mazatlan
Fish/seafood

Plaza Financiera, 9542 Boulevard Sanchez Taboada
Zona Rio, Tijuana   84-88-82 or 84-88-83

Daily 10 am-11 pm   Moderate

The merits are a gorgeous dining room, an extensive menu with English translations, and fresh fish and seafood. Preparations are simple. The price of the main course includes an appetizer, seafood soup, and Mexican rolls. Pleasant experience.

Signature Dishes: Abalone, squid, crab, clams, shrimp, and lobster.

Take Paseo de los Héroes until you come to the second circle. At the second circle you will see a bank, Bancomer. Make a right. Go one block, make another right,. After one-half block you will be at Plaza Financiera. The restaurant is at the front of the Plaza.

El Rodeo
Beef and steaks

1647 Boulevard Salinas, Tijuana   86-56-40

Daily 11-11   Moderate

Steak lovers will have a field day here. Vaquero (cowboy) decor.
Signature Dishes: Steak in a variety of cuts, some cooked right
at your table. The accompaniments are wonderful: appetizer and
quesadilla, crisp salad, beans, and dessert are included in the
price of an entrée. Excellent cheese soup, burritos, and tripe.

Take Revolución until it bends to the left to become Agua
Caliente; proceed past the twin high-rise towers. Turn left, and
left again, onto the one-way street, Boulevard Salinas. El Rodeo
is highly visible on the right side.

El Tablon
Beef, fowl

Boulevard Sanchez Taboada and Ninth Street
(No street number) Zona Rio, Tijuana   84-73-32

Daily 7 am-11 pm   Low to low moderate

Good, clean, low-cost dining room. Complete meals—appetizer,
soup, entrée—cost from $8-15.
Signature Dishes: Grilled steak and chicken.

This restaurant is across the street from the fruit and vegetable
market in Zona Rio. See beginning of this chapter for directions.

El Taurino
Beef, fish

7531 Sixth Street (off Revolución), Tijuana   85-70-75

Daily 11 am-12 midnight   Low to moderate, except lobster

Gorgeous room in the heart of old Tijuana, three blocks west of
Revolución. Entrée price includes grilled quail, soup or salad,
and mammoth main course. The maitre d' speaks perfect English.
Signature Dishes: Steak, fish, seafood, and fowl. Almost
everyone orders *cabreria* (grilled filet of New York-cut steak) or
empapelado (fish and shrimp cooked in silver foil). Fresh
lobsters are another good bet.

Follow the sign marked "Centro" ("Downtown") to Third Street
where you see Revolución. Use fee parking on Fifth Street.

La Casa De Alfonso Estaban Cantu
Spanish,
2007 Colonia Davila
Basque
Tijuana
81-89-55

M-Sat 1 pm-12 midnight   Moderate to expensive

Don't miss this outstanding Basque and Spanish restaurant. I actually kissed the chef's hand. Highly romantic setting and gorgeous food.

Signature Dishes: *Cabrito* (roasted baby goat); *camarones Costa Brava* (shrimp topped with pimentos, chiles, and tomatoes). *Bacalao*, paella, and fish stew are also available.

Take Paseo de los Héroes at the border, driving past the Cultural Center and Plaza Fiesta until you see Ensenada Libre. Turn right at this sign, cross two stoplights. At the building called Marco Disco, turn right and at the next corner, turn left. The restaurant is immediately to the left.

La Costa
Fish/seafood
8131 Galeana (Seventh Street between Revolución
    and Constitución)
Tijuana
85-84-94 or 85-31-24

Daily 10 am-12 midnight   Low moderate to moderate

An extensive menu, fresh product, and huge portions have made La Costa the reigning seafood house. Prices here are lower than at the brother restaurant, Adrian Pedrin. Cost of entrées includes soup, salad, rice, dessert, beverage, and after-dinner drink. Almost always crowded.

Signature Dishes: Lobster, shrimp, grilled fish, fish with sauces, squid, abalone, and oysters.

Follow the sign marked "Centro" ("Downtown") to Third Street to Revolución and Seventh Street. Easy to find.

La Escondido
International, Mexican

1 Santa Monica, Fraccionamiento Las Palmas
Tijuana   81-44-58

Daily 8 am-1 am   Moderate

"The Hidden One," located in a converted mansion, boasts two gardens and patio dining, and is especially beautiful at night. Piano player on F and Sat.

Signature Dishes: Caesar salad; bone marrow or oxtail soups; roasted baby goat; quail; and Chateaubriand steak (for two). Dishes with sauces are not as satisfying as those that are charbroiled or roasted.

Take Revolución until it bends to the left to become Agua Caliente. Proceed on Agua Caliente past the racetrack, approximately half a mile. Turn right at Las Palmas. Two short blocks up, turn left at the "Pasteleria/Navy" sign. The entrance to La Escondido is straight ahead.

La Espadaña
Meat, seafood

10813 Avenida Sanchez Taboada
Zona Rio, Tijuana   34-14-88 or 34-14-89

Daily 7:30 am-11 pm   Moderate

Beautifully prepared meals include appetizer, soup or salad, and entrée. Mammoth portions; delightful atmosphere. The building resembles a mission. Menus printed in Spanish and English. Some English spoken.

Signature Dishes: *Brocheta de filete* (filet steak on a skewer); *costillar de puerco* (baby back ribs); *camarones con champinones* (shrimp and mushrooms in butter sauce); *pierna de borrego* (leg of lamb).

See instructions at the beginning of this chapter to reach Avenida Sanchez Taboada.

La Fonda Roberto's
Mexican, Puebla style
La Sierra Motel, 16 Avenida de Septiembre
(old road to Ensenada)
Tijuana   86-46-87

Tu-Sun 12 noon-10   Low to moderate

Regional specialties. Portions are small, so two people may wish
to order three entrées.

Signature Dishes: Beef tongue in sesame seed sauce; spicy
shredded pork with artichoke seeds; two preparations of chicken;
a half dozen steak dishes. Don't miss the soups or *chile en nogada*
(chile filled with meat and fruit, covered with white sauce).

Take the Old Ensenada Highway to Agua Caliente Blvd.; the sign
there reads, "Blvd. Cuauhtemoc Suroeste." Roberto's is in the
motel just after the road veers right.

La Leña
Beef, fowl
4560 Boulevard Agua Caliente
Tijuana   86-29-20

Daily 12 noon-12 midnight   Moderate

The most fastidious American will feel comfortable here. Dinner
comes w. appetizer and soup.

Signature Dishes: *Puños* (marinated beef that's roasted and
combined with ham, pork, large grilled green onions, and melted
cheese); *gaonera* (meat pounded thin, stuffed with guacamole,
beans, or cheese). Excellent quail and chicken.

Take Revolución to the left-hand bend where it becomes Agua
Caliente. Continue past the twin towers of the Fiesta Americana.
A large sign marks the restaurant (on the right).

La Taberna Española
Spanish *tapas*

Plaza Fiesta, 9415 Paseo de los Héroes
Zona Rio, Tijuana   84-75-62

W-M 1-12 midnight   Low

If Spanish appetizers appeal to you, there's no better spot than
this tiny *tapas* bar. Though the menu is in Spanish, one waiter
speaks excellent English. Invariably crowded.

Signature Dishes: The *tapas* are outstanding yet inexpensive.

Take Paseo de los Héroes to the Cultural Center. Plaza Fiesta is
across the street on the right.

Las Carnes
Steak house

10471 Paseo de los Héroes
Zona Rio, Tijuana   34-27-21

Daily 1 -roughly 12 midnight   Low to low moderate

Immaculate restaurant; limited menu. One steak order serves two
or three; it's best with a side order of grilled green onions and
sautéed white onions, or roasted chiles. Don't be talked into too
much steak. Swift, streamlined service.

Signature Dishes: Thin, grilled steak called *cabreria*—plus half
a dozen side dishes.

Take Paseo de los Héroes at the border.

Las Espuelas
International

Centro Rio Plaza (opposite the Tijuana Cultural Center
on Paseo de los Héroes), Tijuana   84-01-57

Daily 8 am-11 pm   Moderate

Close to the cultural center. Fresh but unexciting food. The
atmosphere rates high, as does the service. Lunch specials are
the best buys, and so is breakfast.

Signature Dishes: Chicken, steak, and quail are good,
particularly if you order them without sauces.

Take Paseo de los Héroes to the Cultural Center. Centro Rio Plaza
is opposite the Cultural Center.

Mr. Fish
Fish/seafood

6000 Boulevard Agua Caliente
Tijuana   86-36-03

Sun-Th 12 noon-10; F-Sat 12 noon-11
Moderate

It's fun to eat in this restaurant with its thatched roof. The crepe preparations are wild—there's even a Mexican version of blintzes.

Signature Dishes: Oysters; whole fish (steamed or fried) or filet in garlic butter. If you'd like a smorgasbord, the "Combination Mr. Fish" supplies fresh lobster, shrimp, squid, and filet of fish.

Follow Revolución until it bends to the left and becomes Agua Caliente. Continue past the twin high-rise towers. Mr. Fish is on the right, just before the country club.

Pedrin's
Fish/seafood

1115 Avenida Revolución (opposite the Jai Alai palace)
Tijuana   85-40-52

Daily 10 am-12 midnight   Moderate

The dining room has a city view, and the menu offers over 50 fish and seafood items reminiscent of those at Pedrin's brother restaurant, La Costa. The price of an entrée includes appetizer, soup, salad, nonalcoholic beverage, and after-dinner drink.

Signature Dishes: Combination plates; whole, boneless, charcoal-broiled fish; whole fish in garlic sauce; broiled lobster; shrimp baked with spinach.

Follow the sign marked "Centro" ("Downtown") to Third Street to Revolución. Continue south on Revolución until you see the Jai Alai Palace.

Tour de France   French, Spanish
252 Gobernador Ibarra (past the Rio section)
Tijuana   81-75-42

M-Th 1:30-10:30; F-Sat 1:30-11:30   Moderate to expensive

This French restaurant provides wonderful food, incredible service, and an extensive menu printed in French, Spanish, and English. The food is first-rate. Reservations a must on weekends. Dressy.

Signature Dishes: Escargots in puff pastry; salmon in olive sauce; duck in fig sauce; steaks. Don't miss the desserts, especially the chestnut soufflé.

Phone for directions. English is spoken. It's one of the best restaurants in Tijuana, but you have to follow driving instructions. Take Paseo de los Héroes and turn right at the second traffic circle (the one with the Indian). Continue three blocks to Agua Caliente Blvd., turn left, and in two blocks turn left again onto Gobernador Ibarra. Continue one block; Tour de France is behind the Palacio Azteca Hotel.

Viviana Restaurant   Duck, beef
10092 Boulevard Agua Caliente (directly across from
    the bull ring)
Tijuana   81-70-85 or 86-37-53

Daily 12 noon-12 midnight   Moderate to expensive

An upscale restaurant with tableside preparations, table telephones, and glossy interior. Some Continental-style dishes are too elaborate. Excellent service; valet parking.

Signature Dishes: Superb duck and beef dishes. If you arrive with a large party, order an entire duck and have the chef carve it. Filet steaks also do well here.

Take Revolución to Agua Caliente to the bull ring.

General Dining Tip: Many people are fond of all-you-can-eat buffets. Please bear in mind that food placed in steam tables grows soggy. Arrive early for any buffet. No meal is a bargain if the items sit around too long.

Patio Dining

Late-night Dining

Bargain Dining

Dancing

Music

Specialties

AFGHAN

AMERICAN